MR. ROOSEVELT'S
STEAMBOAT

Also by Mary Helen Dohan
OUR OWN WORDS

MR. ROOSEVELT'S STEAMBOAT

by
Mary Helen Dohan

DODD, MEAD & COMPANY
New York

Library of Congress Cataloging in Publication Data

Dohan, Mary Helen.
  Mr. Roosevelt's steamboat.

  Bibliography: p.
  Includes index.
  1.   Mississippi River—Description and travel.
2.   Mississippi Valley—Description and travel.
3.   Roosevelt, Nicholas J., 1767–1854.   4.   Steam-navigation—Mississippi
River—History—19th century.   5.   New Orleans (Steamboat)   I. Title.
F353.D57   917.7'042   81-5488
ISBN 0-396-07983-0   AACR2

Remembering Stasia, my mother—
her vibrant spirit, her questing mind

ILLUSTRATIONS

MAPS

Early in our industrial history this valley was the seat of the largest development of inland navigation in the United States; and perhaps you will pardon my mentioning that the first steamboat west of the Alleghanies [sic] was built by a Roosevelt, my great-grandfather's brother, in 1811, for the New Orleans trade, and in that year made the trip from Pittsburgh to New Orleans.

—*Theodore Roosevelt, in a speech made at the Deep Waterway Convention at Memphis, Tennessee, October 4, 1907*

PREFACE

The story of the steamboat *New Orleans*, the first to challenge the western rivers, is one of many versions. The vessel has been described as a side-wheeler and as a stern-wheeler, as carrying one hundred tons or four hundred, as having this measurement or that. About dates, places, and the duration of her historic voyage everyone is sure but few agree. Even the primary source of all accounts, that of John H. B. Latrobe, Lydia Roosevelt's half-brother, who told the story as he heard it from her, contains demonstrable errors.

From many sources, however, it has been possible to reconstruct forgotten aspects of the voyage. New evidence settles some long-disputed issues. And Nicholas and Lydia Roosevelt, who together braved those rivers, come alive in materials only recently disclosed. All that I tell of them, therefore, the man, the woman, and the boat, is consistent with evidence painstakingly unearthed.

My quest for facts about the vessel, the voyage, and the Roosevelts themselves has led me to many individuals, as well as to historical societies, libraries, and museums. It has introduced me to the fraternity of waterways professionals and steamboat buffs, bound together by an extraordinary mystique. It has brought me into contact with members of the Roosevelt family, whose pride in their ancestry reflects generations of leadership and achievement, and with Latrobe descendants, equally proud.

Cornelius Van S. Roosevelt has long been interested in his three times great-granduncle Nicholas and in the steamboat. Not only did he allow me the use of his correspondence with such river authorities as Captain Frederick Way, Jr., but also provided me with genealogical data on the Roosevelt family. Henry Hoff, Nicholas and Lydia's direct descendant and himself a genealogist, helped me enormously in locating family members and other likely sources, as did James Roosevelt of Oyster Bay, who is presently updating the Roosevelt genealogy. Mr. and Mrs. William Morrow Roosevelt, of Fort Washington, Pennsylvania, very kindly took snapshots for my use of their portrait of Lydia, published here for the first time.

On the Latrobe side, Mrs. Samuel Wilson, Jr., of New Orleans, and Mrs. Gamble Latrobe, of Wilmington, Delaware, searched through family records for memorabilia of Lydia, their half several times great-aunt. Actually, it was a Latrobe record, the published letters of Benjamin Henry Latrobe, Lydia's father, that presented me with the scenario for Nicholas Roosevelt's mid-life career and his tempestuous courtship. It is my good fortune that Edward C. Carter, II, of the Maryland Historical Society, has collected and edited them so superbly.

John Briley, of the Campus Martius Museum in Marietta, Ohio, answered many of my amateur's questions about early steamboats. Nellie Carstens, of the Filson Club, in Louisville, Kentucky, searched out valuable materials relating to the Great Comet of 1811 and to the steamboat's visit to Louisville. Michael Newton Samsot drew the excellent map of the New Madrid Area Rift Zone especially for this book. I appreciate particularly the help given me by Wallace Dailey, curator of the Theodore Roosevelt Collection at Harvard University; by William Emerson, director of the Franklin D. Roosevelt Library at Hyde Park; and by John Gable, director of the Theodore Roosevelt Association *xii* at Oyster Bay, in locating pertinent materials from their special collections. Richard Wright, president of the Onondaga Historical Association, in Syracuse, New York; John Stinson, of the New York Public Library Manuscripts and Archives Department; Thomas Dunnings of the New-York Historical Society; Ruth S. Reid of the Historical Society of Western Pennsylvania; and Tina H. Sheller of the Maryland Historical Society have been generous in their assistance. Others who contributed useful information or documents are Robert F. Cayton, of the Dawes Memorial Library of Marietta College; Laura L. Chace of the Cincinnati Historical Society; Catherine Barnes and Helen W. Ionta, local historians of Skaneateles, New York; Jill Tempest of the Judge George W. Armstrong Library in Natchez, Mississippi,; Melissa Payne, of the Louisiana Maritime Museum; and the staffs of the Louisiana section of the New Orleans Public Library and of Tulane University, especially Margery Wylie of the latter.

The loving encouragement of my husband, Robert D. Samsot, and of the rest of my family has made my quest a joyous one. And Margaret Norton, my editor at Dodd, Mead, has been the ideal editor, ready with counsel but not precept, enthusiastic and a friend.

To all of these I am grateful.

1

Like a quickening wind, excitement ruffled the crowd gathered
on the banks of the Monongahela at Pittsburgh on the twentieth
day of October in 1811. It rippled across gossiping clusters of
the fashionably dressed—women in spencers of velvet or lute-
string and gently falling skirts or in fur-lined tippets over walking dress, men in narrow pantaloons with gaiters or soft leather
boots, whose high collars and folded neckcloths gave them a sore-
throated look. It passed on to others, less stylishly dressed, who
stood a little apart, women in full-skirted dresses and shawls
pulled tight against the chill and men in wider pantaloons and
jackets of deplorable line. Finally, it skipped over to the red-
shirted rivermen in buckskins who stood scowling and spitting
tobacco along the river bank, flicking at them until they too
stirred beneath its touch.

Latecomers felt the excitement as they hurried along Wood
Street or Grant beneath the bordering poplars or turned in from
Market Street, sidestepping mud holes and the scavenging pigs
that poked at garbage and dead cats. So did those who drifted
in from Braddock's Field Road to join the eager procession making its way toward Water Street. For here, in the valley beneath   *1*

Boyd's Hill, near Suke's Run, lay the shops and yards of the Mississippi Steamboat Navigation Company; and here, on this bright Sunday morning, one could view the departure of Mr. Nicholas Roosevelt's steamboat, the *New Orleans,* first to challenge the dangerous western waters, on her maiden—some said her one and only—voyage.

Voices rose and fell along the riverbank and up the hill; here and there was laughter, and the shrill shouts of children floated on the crisp October air. Spectators craned their necks for a better view of the river, where the blue-hulled steamboat huffed and puffed and blew black smoke like a squat, contemplative dragon. One hundred forty-eight and a half feet long and thirty-two and a half wide, with a molded depth of twelve feet, she loomed large to eyes more used to flats and keelboats and even to giant barges. Her curious paddle wheels poked out on either side, her dark chimney was tall as a manufactory's, and the tapered masts, fore and aft, reached toward a smoke-smudged sky.

Not all the attention was on the boat. Heads turned too to watch the pathway leading to the shipyard office, from which twenty-year-old Lydia Roosevelt, eight months pregnant, would soon emerge with her little girl. Some of the voices raised were sharp, incredulous: "Is she really going?" "She did before, didn't she?" "Yes, but with the *child*—" (Some said *bairn,* and some said *daft,* too, in the "braid Scots" so much heard in Pittsburgh.) It was clear from the comments exchanged that many of those who were there were dubious about the propriety of Mrs. Roosevelt's presence aboard the vessel, dubious too about her husband's good judgment and even his sense of decency. For a year and a half, though, the boat-loving people of Pittsburgh had watched the *New Orleans* a-building, and most of them felt that both the boat and the Roosevelts, Easterners though they were, deserved a fine farewell. Especially fine, considering that once they made their perilous way downriver (if they actually did), the boat at least would never return. She was scheduled to ply as a packet between her namesake city and Natchez, whence goods could travel upriver by keelboat or over the Natchez Trace.

There were some sorrowful faces in the crowd. The Roosevelts had become a part of the community during their lengthy stay, and there were those among the spectators, wise in the rivers' ways, who saw trouble ahead. Reaching Louisville, with its shallow, treacherous falls, where a deep-hulled vessel could wait months for a rise, would be the easy part; if the rapids were successfully passed—a big *if*—there lay between the scattered settlements along the Ohio long stretches of forbidding wilderness. Within them lurked remnants of murderous pirate gangs and vicious boat wreckers. Indians in the region, relatively quiet for a generation, were being newly stirred to anger by the calls for war of Tecumseh, chief of the Shawnees, who sought to unite tribes north and south in a great confederacy. His passionate eloquence, supported by the awe his followers felt for his brother, called the Prophet, threatened the interior lands with a bloody and terrible war. Below the Ohio, along the Mississippi, where the unsettled shores extended for hundreds of miles and Indian tribes still held formal possession of much of the land, the dangers would be greater still; and little help could be looked for from settlers along the way. Only New Madrid on the western side and Natchez on the east were more than tiny villages; and settlers occupying the old Spanish land grants to the west in what was now Louisiana Territory were few and widely scattered. They were not generally sympathetic to "Americans" either, even though, since the Purchase eight years earlier, that was what they themselves were supposed to be (to the distress of Easterners, who saw in the Purchase not only extravagant folly but a charter for mischief against the established states).

Then, as if man-made dangers were not enough, there lay in wait for rash mortals the "wicked river" itself, with its snags and bars and deadly ripples, a hostile, elemental force, jealous and vengeful, its allies the wind and the sky and the very earth. To float submissively along on its shifting currents by flatboat or keelboat was one thing, a venture that offered no defiance to stir the river's wrath, or to push laboriously upward month after month, paying appropriate tribute in muscle and skill and a measure of fear, but to challenge the Mississippi in an impudent, untried boat with a roaring boiler sure to explode and paddles flapping along the sides was the act of a fool—and a fool's wife.

Lydia Roosevelt had no more sense than her husband, 3

Map from *Travels on an Inland Voyage, Performed in the Years 1807 and 1808. New York 1810*

Voyage of the New Orleans

everyone said, despite her being the eldest daughter of the distinguished architect Benjamin Latrobe, surveyor general of the United States, whom one would expect to have some influence on her. One would expect it, that is, who did not know how little influence he had had in trying to stop her marriage to a man more than twice her age and—New York Roosevelt or not—an evidently improvident one as well. Nor had he been able to dissuade her from going along on that impossible flatboat voyage two years ago, in 1809, a voyage that she and her husband called a belated honeymoon but that most sensible people agreed only showed her willfulness.

It was a survey voyage assigned to Roosevelt by his partners, Messrs. Fulton and Livingston. On it they were to base their decision about the feasibility of building a steamboat for the western waters. One could hardly believe that either Robert Livingston, former chancellor of New York and minister to France, or Robert Fulton, whose *North River Steamboat of Clermont* was even now marvelously plying the Hudson River, expected him to take his bride along and make a six-months' sightseeing voyage of the assignment, not to speak of spending their money to open coal mines along the way for fuel for a boat that had yet to be built. Roosevelt had a reputation for getting into financial trouble by just such impetuous ways, always blithely assuming that somebody else would pick up the tab. A splendid maker of steam engines but notorious for financial failures and currently in debt up to his ears, he had been taken in as a third partner in the Pittsburgh venture at the behest of Mr. Latrobe, who was friendly with Fulton and hoped the project would bring good fortune not only for Roosevelt's sake and his daughter's, but also for his own. He had unwisely endorsed a number of Roosevelt's notes, still unpaid, when Roosevelt had been his friend and partner but not yet his son-in-law.

Few people in Pittsburgh, though, knew much about the marriage or how it came about. Few of them even knew the Latrobes or the Roosevelts, Easterners all, but they did know about the flatboat voyage, for it was in Pittsburgh that it began. And used as they were in this frontier town to the unconventional, Lydia Roosevelt had managed to shock even them.

They had not yet become prudes, these Westerners—frontier living was too immediate, too close—but even here a defensive reaction to British disdain for American culture and manners was creating an artificial social code. The rising affluence in the cities that was making female idleness possible and the idle wife a symbol of success was promoting an exaggerated ideal of the "lady," and traditional respect for the working woman was disappearing. Even for the frontier wife, the ultimate goal of the arduous struggle for survival was to attain a society in which the struggle would no longer be needed and gentility would prevail. The piano carted laboriously across the mountains, the silk dress dreamed of, the useless ornament treasured were earnest of an easeful, gentle life to come. Especially in proud western towns like Pittsburgh and Cincinnati, decorum among the "ladies" was carried to extremes that amused visitors from abroad or from the more sophisticated East. Someone like Lydia Roosevelt, daughter of a distinguished family, stepdaughter of lovely Mary Hazlehurst Latrobe, who was Dolley Madison's dear friend, and wife of a man whose family name was known even in Pittsburgh, was expected to keep the lady image bright. To do less was to betray not only her sex but her country too.

She'd not cared at all. Not only had she insisted on going along on the flatboat trip like an ordinary frontier woman (taking a maid along, however); not only had the voyage lasted six months; not only had she and her husband slept often in the open with all the crew about; not only did she herself, when fever struck everyone else aboard, clean and cook and nurse the sick (including the filthy hired hands) for three whole weeks, once bailing out the boat from nine in the evening until one in the morning—that was not all. No, the most shocking aspect of the whole voyage was that, during the entire time, Lydia Roosevelt was, visibly for the most part, pregnant. She and her husband had barely made it back to New York from New Orleans, on a ship with yellow fever aboard, in time for the baby to be born.

So what could one expect now? What one ought *rightly* to expect, the matrons of Pittsburgh said to one another—and although the words of most came out as soft expressions of distress, those of some were hurled like stones—was that her husband 7 would put his foot down this time. After all, she was in a family way again, and the insistence of the two of them on being together even now was—well, strange. Their husbands, if they knew Mr. Roosevelt well enough, remonstrated delicately with him after a wink and a clap on the back intended to show that they understood how it was to be married to a girl twenty-three years younger (and how was it? they wondered), but the remonstrances were for the most part kindly. Not only were many of those who spoke to him personal friends; they were also aware of what the building of the *New Orleans* had meant to Pittsburgh in dollars and cents. The work of construction had called for the services and products of foundries and shops; there were jobs at the boatyard for carpenters and joiners and caulkers; expert mechanics were brought in from the East to work on the construction of the engine; and a number of local enterprises—a rolling mill, forges, a slitting mill, a rope walk, machine shops—were projected in response to the promise of a whole new industry. Mr. Roosevelt had shown his own confidence in the future of Pittsburgh by investing in a distillery and a snuffbox factory right here in town.

Besides, they were an attractive couple, even if at first you might take them for father and daughter. They were welcomed at once into Pittsburgh's small elite, to be entertained by the O'Haras and Nevilles and Rosses, the Bateses and Baldwins and Scotts—die-hard Federalists and Republicans alike—and to entertain nicely themselves. True, they were not Presbyterians, but one could make allowances for that. They had many local connections. Albert Gallatin, former congressman from western Pennsylvania and now secretary of the treasury, was the Latrobes' neighbor in Washington. Aaron Burr, who had been instrumental in bringing statehood to Tennessee and who was still popular in the West (no one mourned Alexander Hamilton, instigator of the infamous whisky tax), had been for years a close family friend. Here in Pittsburgh, Benjamin Bakewell, whose glassworks was located almost adjacent to the boatyard, was the uncle of Mrs. Roosevelt's Philadelphia friend Lucy Bakewell, who had married a handsome Frenchman named John James Audubon and

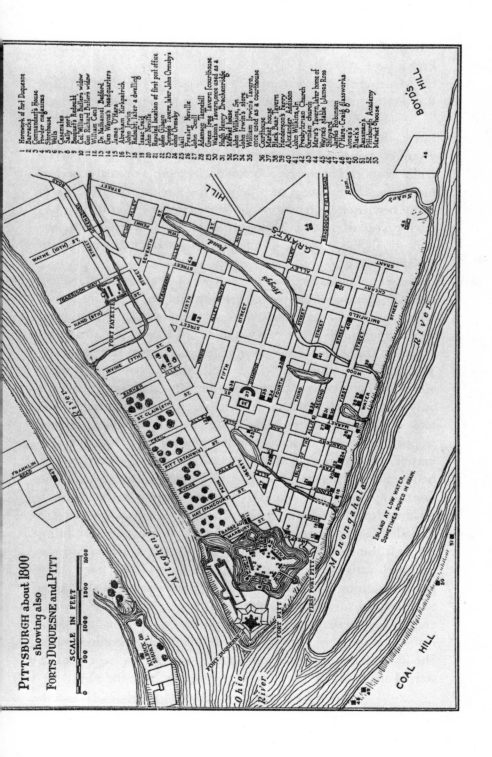

PITTSBURGH about 1800
showing also
FORTS DUQUESNE and PITT

SCALE IN FEET

0   500   1000   1500   2000

1   Hornwork of Fort Duquesne
2   Barracks
3   Commandant's House
4   Powder magazines
5   Storehouse
6   Wells
7   Casemates
8   Sally port
9   Bouquet's Redoubt
10 Col William Butler's widow
11 Gen Richard Butler's widow
12 William Cecil
13 Dr. Nathaniel Bedford
14 Gen Wayne's headquarters
15 James O'Hara
16 Abraham Kirkpatrick
17 John Irwin
18 Redoubt, later a dwelling
19 Isaac Craig
20 John Neville
21 Reputed location of first post office
22 John Gibson
23 Semple's Tavern, later John Ormsby's
24 John Ormsby
25 Presley Neville
26 John Scull
27 Adamson Tannehill
28 Green Tree Tavern [courthouse
29 Watson's Tavern, once used as a
30 Hugh Henry Brackenridge
31 Morrell house
32 John Wilkins, Sn
33 John Irwin's store
34 William Irwin's Tavern,
35 once used as a courthouse
36 Courthouse
37 Market house
38 Black Bear Tavern
39 Henderson's Ferry
40 Alexander Addison
41 John Wilkins, Jr.
42 Presbyterian Church
43 German church
44 Marie's Tavern, later home of
45 Wayne's stable [James Ross
46 Shippen Road
47 James Robinson
48 O'Hara Craig glassworks
49 James Ross
50 Bausman's
51 Bausman's
52 Pittsburgh Academy
53 Market house

was now living in Henderson, Kentucky, where her husband kept a store.

During those weeks prior to the flatboat trip, therefore, the Roosevelts visited in James Ross's sumptuous Georgian-style home near Aspinwall and at the clapboard homes on Market Street, for which the "Clapboard Junta," a powerful political group of merchants and professional men, was named. They attended concerts of the Apollonian Society and a dramatic performance in which young men played the female roles, and made many new friends. It was natural that after their return the following year from New York with Rosetta Mark Roosevelt, the cause of all the clucking of tongues, they were soon involved in Pittsburgh life.

Lydia often walked with Rosetta down to the Point, where the Allegheny and the Monongahela meet to form the broad Ohio, there to see the vessels loading and unloading, arriving and departing, and hear the sweet sound of the boathorn as a vessel rounded the bend. She went marketing with her maid on Wednesdays and Saturdays, traveled by hired carriage out to the scenes of the curious rock carvings not far from town (there was only one private carriage in Pittsburgh, Mr. O'Hara's). She looked over the books in Mr. Patterson's new bookstore, and stopped in for mail at the post office where John Scull, the postmaster, printed the *Gazette* in a back room of his two-story log house. She learned to lift her skirts in the street and from the floor in any public place and to control her temper when tobacco juice spattered her dress, and to stand aside for the coach from Philadelphia or the huge Conestoga wagons that came rumbling through the streets on their iron-tired wheels, as well as for the pigs and goats that seemed to own the streets—but, then, they did in Washington, too! She kept only river water in the house for drinking, for the spring water was impregnated with coal oil, and she kept a wary eye for dogs with frothing mouths. Not even madstones could save anyone, once bitten, from a horrible death. She learned, too, not to argue politics, not only because politics started sparks flying but also because women here did not.

10   And she visited the boatyard. She had inspected the cabin

specifications with a designer's eye (had she not designed the flatboat interior? and very well too!) and loved watching the steamboat take shape. She knew that her boatyard visits were sometimes criticized by other women, whose activities rarely encroached on their husbands' domains, and knew that their husbands believed the visits set a bad precedent—a man should have one woman-free place in his life—but in her role as young mother she had gained rapport with the women, and their husbands simply liked her. She was lively and bright and pretty, with a charming way of gesticulating that seemed interestingly French, and older men, who felt awkward initially with this wife of their contemporary who was herself younger than their daughters, soon found themselves at ease. They looked in vain for the defects in Mrs. Roosevelt's features that a few of the wives had pointed out to them.

Interest in the Roosevelts, however, was more than equalled by interest in the *New Orleans*. Pittsburgh was supremely boat-conscious. For a while it had even turned out seagoing ships, but now the building of keelboats and flatboats, barges and packets alone kept the riverfront yards constantly busy. It was to those boatyards that men came who wanted the best, who knew that here was the knowledge of the rivers' demands and the skills to make boats that could meet them. Here, eight years earlier, the boatwatchers watched as Meriwether Lewis's custom-built keelboat took shape for the great expedition to the West, with its ten-foot decks at bow and stern, its forecastle and cabin and movable breastworks. Here too they watched as barges of all sizes and shapes were made, often of fifty-ton burden or more, designed to carry forty hands besides the patroon, or captain. They saw pass along the Ohio all manner of boats bearing people and things: trading boats, with their calico flags; keelboats heavy with pine planks brought by wagon from New York or with furs from Maine or with Philadelphia flour; broadhorns and ferryflats and Allegheny skiffs; floating grist mills and tobacco boats; showboats; family boats—these last, many of them, homemade and in such wondrous shapes that a traveler wrote for history that one could "scarcely imagine an abstract form in which a boat can   *11* be built, that in some part of the Ohio or Mississippi you will not see, actually in motion." But for even the finest, the sleekest of boats, one round trip a year to New Orleans was the best that could be done.

This limitation was mightily pleasing to the eastern merchants, who wished no competition from a busy inland trade. As it was, the Westerners were kept comfortably in debt to them by means of nine to twelve months credit terms for products wagoned in from Philadelphia or Baltimore or New York while their own products traveled slowly downriver once a year. The profitable trans-Atlantic trade carried on by eastern merchant fleets often consisted of western products—lumber and flour and whisky—that were carted into eastern ports, bought at low prices, and sold for enormous profit at European ports. The East knew that if those western products, the superior western flour, for instance, that sold in New Orleans for a dollar more than any other, came down the river in greater volume or more speedily, to be shipped on to the West Indies and elsewhere, it could displace what arrived by sea from Baltimore and Philadelphia. It might even travel up the seaboard and create a demand for it where eastern flour had a gratifying monopoly.

It was the thought of those eastern merchants that could bring a Westerner's blood to a boil. Western Pennsylvanians felt with a sense of mission that Pittsburgh was appointed to become the Birmingham of America and the Gateway to the West. From the beginning of settlement, there had been no nonsense about religion: the early settlers had come here for economic reasons or to escape the Revolution, and only ministers very recently arrived assailed the notion that business came first. The archenemy of that mission was the breeches-wearing, Federalist-leaning eastern establishment, made up of a combination of Shylocks and greedy merchants determined to keep for themselves not only the balance of trade but the political power that went with it.

"The old states sink," Josiah Quincy of Massachusetts cried angrily as new western lands were opened. What right had Congress to dilute the power of the original thirteen? New Englanders proclaimed the Louisiana Purchase a disaster, unconstitutional and extravagant. Before you knew it, they predicted

12

gloomily, the destiny of the nation would be in the hands of wild men from Missouri and other barbaric lands. If new states were formed from Louisiana Territory, New England, her spokesmen threatened, might well secede, "amicably if possible, violently if necessary," to form with New York an independent nation as was their right under the compact of sovereign states.

For their part, western Pennsylvanians in particular saw on every hand the nefarious work of their enemies. Even now, with the first digging for the National Road taking place, there was talk in Congress of establishing its first junction not at Pittsburgh, a natural point of departure for the West, but at Wheeling, which just happened to be in the state of Virginia. A blind man could see the fine hand of Madison in that! The *Gazette* and the *Commonwealth* lamented the tribute paid by their subscribers to the "Pennsylvania and Maryland waggoners," who took only precious specie from the West and none of its produce. They assailed the indifference of Congress to improving the navigation of the western waters and deplored the lack of concern on the seaboard for the Indian menace on the frontier. They denounced Congress for its refusal to recognize that the British, still hoping to salvage some of America's territory, were fanning the flames of savagery. What good would it do western Pennsylvania, they demanded, to boast of its proliferating factories, of its glassworks and sawmills and distilleries, foundries and boatyards, of its superior flour and excellent rye whisky, as long as transportation remained slow and hazardous and the imbalance of imports mortgaged the region to the traders and bankers of Philadelphia, Baltimore, New York, and Boston?

If, though, the rumor ran, this crazy steamboat idea really worked, if a vessel could go downriver at a speed of eight or ten miles an hour—an hour, mind you!—and upstream at three or four, even against the Mississippi, as opposed to the three miles an hour down and (with luck) the mile an hour upstream of a barge, it would revolutionize trade in favor of the West. The Mississippi, that great, wicked river was, as Madison once said, ". . . to them [Westerners] everything . . . the Hudson, the Delaware, the Potomac, and all the navigable rivers of the Atlantic States, formed into one stream." With steamboats it could *13* carry three or four times its present burden. Products from factory and farm—surplus salt and beef and flour and apples, guns and cordage and whisky and cotton—would go racing down the Ohio to the big river and on to New Orleans, and from there to the West Indies, to Europe, up the coast to eastern ports, to ports all over the world. Furs from the far Northwest, where John Jacob Astor now had a trading center, would travel down the Missouri more quickly than ever before. With ready access to markets, settlers would move into the interior, land would become more valuable; they would build homes, shops, factories, towns, cities. There would be new states—a region could fill up with the required thirty thousand people in no time, and the West would have other men in Congress like Henry Clay and Albert Gallatin. *Then* the uppity East would get its comeuppance. Maybe the United States of America would start looking westward the way they should; maybe there would even be a real feeling of union. St. Louis might become the national capital.

Even before the keel of the *New Orleans* was laid, therefore, the yard of the Mississippi Steamboat Navigation Company was a magnet for sightseers. Men would stop by after a day's work was done or stroll with their wives along Water Street on Sunday and climb Boyd's Hill to look down on the scene. Small boys, drawn as flies to honey to the construction site, pestered the workmen and got to know Tiger, the Roosevelts' great Labrador, who came often with his mistress to visit the yard. Visitors from the East asked as often, it seemed, to see "Mr. Roosevelt's boat" as they did to visit the glass factories that were Pittsburgh's pride.

It was not actually Mr. Roosevelt's boat, and it was reported that the tendency of people to call it his was extremely annoying to his associates, especially Robert Fulton, who designed it. Roosevelt was the least prestigious and certainly the poorest of the partners, but here he was the most visible. It was fortunate for the success of the project that he was, for Messrs. Fulton and Livingston were anything but popular in the region. They had tried to obtain from the states along the way the same monopoly for the western rivers that they held for the Hudson, by which they

and they alone would have the right to use steam for navigation along those rivers for twenty years. This in the West!—where whatever bound, held back, suppressed, was and ever would be anathema. The papers shouted outrage:

> Our road to market must and *will* be free; this monopolizing disposition of individuals will only arouse the citizens of the West to insist on and obtain recognition of their rights, viz. the privilege of passing and repassing, unmolested, on the *common highway* of the West.

Today, the Mississippi; tomorrow it could be lakes or streams or grazing lands. Only Governor Claiborne of the Territory of Orleans, who was not a Westerner, any more than Orleans was the West, had granted them an eighteen-year monopoly after being wooed with a campaign of wining and dining that included a visit to New York and a ride on the *Clermont*. Besides, the greed of them! No wonder Mr. Roosevelt, well liked as he was, had trouble selling subscriptions to the company. Under the conditions of subscription, the partners would divide ninety percent of the profit, with investors receiving dividends from the leftover ten percent. Mr. Roosevelt himself, as he avowed with most engaging candor, had had no part in drawing up the conditions and could hardly be blamed for what he could not control. Besides, he was investing *his* profits locally—in advance of receiving any, it was true; but that he was doing so showed good faith.

Unresponsive as they were to his appeal for investment, therefore, Pittsburgh's citizens had only admiration for Mr. Roosevelt's skill as he went about building the engine and supervising the building of the boat. None knew of the nagging sense of injustice that occasionally beset him. For it was he who had proposed the side paddle wheel design that had made the *Clermont* a brilliant success and that was now being used for the *New Orleans,* a design that had been scoffed at and rejected by Robert Livingston ten years earlier when Roosevelt, employed by him to build a steamboat, had presented the side paddle wheel plan. Later on, or so Roosevelt was convinced, Livingston passed on the side paddle wheel idea to his new found friend and protégé Robert Fulton, who knew a good thing when he saw it and was now reaping the fruits of its execution in glory and wealth.

Moreover, the building of the *New Orleans* went badly. *15*

From the beginning, everything seemed to conspire against its completion. Skeptics were not surprised and the superstitious said that an evil star hung over it already, perhaps the very comet that had appeared so spectacularly in the western sky and that the worldly in their foolishness said had no significance. Already called the Great Comet of 1811, it had streaked into the heavens in March, when the boat was ready for launching, and was visible still, even across the sea. Could anyone think such signs were sent without some purpose?

The boat did seem cursed. To obtain oak for planking was impossible without intolerable delay; white pine had to do, and even that was hard to find. Many splendid old trees in the nearby lowlands had been cut down and shipped downriver as shingles or boards or to be used as masts, and to locate trees of the needed girth and shape and height in the trackless forests was a long and tortuous task. Clearing the chosen area, felling the trees, cutting a path for carting them down to the waiting rafts on the river called for more men, more hours, more pay than the partners had counted on, and Roosevelt's accounts went quickly awry, especially when he increased on his own the boat's dimensions. Available saw pits were old and hardly adequate, and a new one had to be built, as did workshops for joiners and filers and smiths; for lack of a rolling mill in Pittsburgh (one would be built the following year), the boiler plates had to be brought in by ox cart from the East.

There were local boatbuilders aplenty, had been since the turn of the century, when Tarascon, Berthoud, and Company had lured from the East skilled workmen—ship carpenters, joiners, caulkers, riggers—with the promise of higher wages (and how *that* grievance festered in eastern hearts!). However, Roosevelt did import skilled machinists, which was in itself a slap at local pride; when East and West met there were a few sharp words and occasionally fists flew.

And then—! Work had hardly begun when the Monongahela rose, not once but several times. On Sunday, November 11, 1810, in a day and a night the water rose on *both* rivers thirty-seven feet above the common level. The freshet of that date carried off the public wharf on the Allegheny, came within eight feet of Market Street, and ascended Wood Street gutters to Front Street. Penn and Liberty were inundated, and at the boatyard great floods of muddy water came pouring in. All buoyant materials—planks lying in the open for weathering, shaped wood being pruned and puttied and sanded and caulked, scraps of lumber, boxes and barrels and chips—went bobbing about, to the delight of the boys who came sloshing through the water to watch and to the frustration of salvaging crews. During the following months the Monongahela itself rose, again and again as though the great and jealous river to the west had sent word. And when, after all the delays, the hull was nearing completion, a sudden rise almost lifted it from the ways and threatened to launch it prematurely on the swollen stream. It seemed only to be expected that when the boat was finally ready the river was not; months were idled away waiting for the autumn rise.

From all sides, Lydia and Nicholas Roosevelt heard the clucking of tongues and expressions of sympathy, sincere or feigned. It did seem a warning, didn't it? Why couldn't the boat return a profit just making the run to Cincinnati? To Louisville? Did they really expect to take the *New Orleans* over the shallow Falls of the Ohio, at Louisville? Most urgently, why go on that hazardous twenty-five-hundred-mile voyage themselves? There were men paid to take such risks. What had Mr. Roosevelt to gain? Perhaps nothing at all, the rumor went. Pittsburgh businessmen heard from reliable sources that Fulton and Livingston were considering voting him out of his share of the profits because of his continued extravagance. In the shipyard office, clerks who had seen angry letters coming in whispered that Mr. Roosevelt's snuffbox factory and distillery might not have been bought with his own money after all; if they were, they would soon go to pay his debts.

There were other letters that the people of Pittsburgh knew nothing about. Between Lydia and her father had passed a bitter exchange. Latrobe, long exasperated by his son-in-law's disregard for the difficulties he made for everyone else, and feeling personally to blame for Fulton's troubles with him, wrote to his daughter, whose judgment he respected ("I wish Lydia were the husband!" he once exclaimed to her brother), urging her to persuade her husband to mend his ways. The letter was little more than a long critical recounting of Roosevelt's financial dealings and a number of comments upon his reputation as a speculator. Lydia wrote back angrily. Why did her father consent to her marriage, she demanded, if her husband was so devoid of "honor, shame, or feeling"? Why was it that Mr. Fulton could make him believe anything he wanted to about Nicholas? Why couldn't he be *fair*? Lydia was hurt—she loved her father—but about her husband she was fiercely defensive. Nobody, not even Papa, was to criticize him! And to the gossipmongers and the concerned friends in town she responded with a scornful laugh. Ridiculous! she said, when she heard the story of the partners' threat. Why, the profits to come would more than compensate for expenses and would make all the partners rich, once the boat was put into her planned regular run between Natchez and New Orleans.

Once it was—there was the catch. It was strange, murmured the skeptics to one another as they stood beneath the sycamores and looked out toward the blue-hulled vessel that lay puffing away at anchor in midstream, that Fulton and Livingston were not going along. Evidently they felt much as did the people of Pittsburgh, who had left unanswered the *Gazette*'s advertisement soliciting passengers. "Elegant cabin" indeed. What good would that elegant cabin do at the bottom of the river? Or when the boiler exploded and those "unsurpassed accommodations" went up in flames? Another thing, commented a few of the more devout, no good would come of violating the Sabbath by departing this day, even to catch the flood. It was tempting the Lord. Were there not signs enough already that He had tired of man's effrontery? The rivermen were telling dark tales.

It had been a year of omens, a year that would be remembered forever as the Annus Mirabilis of the West. During the earlier months, the great rivers overflowed, and in the wide valley of the Mississippi, from the Missouri to the Gulf, restless waters surged across the banks. Swirling and grumbling, they shouldered their way into low-lying woods, tore at the roots of trees, tumbled them into the stream to make great snags and sawyers for waylaying river boats, clawed relentlessly at the undersides

Model replica of the steamboat *New Orleans,* considered by authorities to be probably the most accurate representation. It was drawn by Robert G. C. Fee, head of the model department at Newport News Shipbuilding Corporation, and built by Robert Thomas of Powhatan Point, Ohio. It is in the Campus Martius Museum, Marietta, Ohio. Courtesy of Ohio Historical Society.

of bluffs to form watery caves. From shallow graves along the shore they washed up the bodies of hastily buried rivermen and rolled them mockingly into murky depths where others like them lay, grim toll of passage on the hungry river.

In the wake of the brown flood, a plague of sickness walked, bringing fever and the deadly flux, and a cruel rash that leaped from settlement to settlement like a flaming visitation. Children sickened, died. Grief hung in the valley like a mist.

Nature itself seemed warped. In the upper valley, it was reported, squirrels gathered by the thousands, by the tens of thousands, answering some mysterious summons. In a solid phalanx they hurried southward, the sound of their chattering so immense that those who heard it stared at one another, unbelieving. By the thousands they perished in the broad Ohio that lay in their path, their rotting carcasses rolling with the stream; the survivors came to rest only when they could go no more.

And then, as if a mighty finger marked that dreadful year, the comet came, splitting the night sky. Its forked and fiery tail seemed an instrument of judgment on which the world would be impaled. Night after night it shed its ghostly light over the forest, turning the velvet dark to a silken gloom. The Shawnees *19* and Chickasaws and Creeks, already restive with the war cries of Tecumseh and his brother the Prophet, which for many months had echoed down the valley, stirred uneasily, fingering their guns. Little wonder that settlers along the river, disoriented, their homes awash and boats aground, spoke in whispers of apocalypse. Crowding into camp meetings called by wandering preachers, they were whipped into frenzy and the inexplicable "jerks" by soaring voices of doom.

But most of Pittsburgh was not devout, and rivermen told tall tales. Moreover, they could well have their own sinister purposes in discouraging the Roosevelts from setting out. To them, sailors of the inland waters, supreme in their domain, the steamboat was an affront. The presumption that steam could do as well as they on the big rivers, or better, derogated their skills, diminished them. The boat would likely fail—everybody knew that. But if, just if, she didn't, then what would become of keelers, of bargers, of the whole wide world, in fact, as man had known it since his first timid ventures upon the waters of the earth? Now the rivermen were indispensable: Vicious as was their reputation, feared as they were in settlements, where their rowdy visits brought bloody rioting, ugly as were the rivalries that left their mark in gouged-out eyes, in bitten-off ears or lips, they could not be spared, and they knew their worth. Responsible for the transportation of cargo and passengers along all the inland waterways, from the forestbound streams of the vast Canadian fur lands to New Orleans itself, they were expected to be ready to row when rowing was needed or to hoist the sails to a breeze; to move quickly and skillfully to avoid boils and eddies and deadly whirlpools and riffles; to carry towlines in hands or teeth to a sometimes hostile shore and haul the boat forward hand over hand; to back the boat, sometimes a hundred feet long or more, away from snags—the deadly planters, tall trees caught firmly by their roots in the bottom of the river, their tops sometimes invisible, and the sawyers, floating trees that moved up and down, up and down with the current and lunged viciously toward unwary vessels. Rivermen had also to be ready to chop a passage through jams of logs and driftwood; to pole up rapids; to warp when necessary, using the towline in reverse; to bushwhack when the river was high, pulling the boat along by grasping the branches of trees along the shore. And to shoot. Boat owners who sought passenger trade included among their inducements not only bulletproof cabins against the hazards of river pirates and Indians but sharpshooters to man them as well. The rivermen filled that role. And now, to have their skills disdained—?

Why should they not be standing there scowling, apart from the restless, gossiping crowd on the river's shore? Those Kaintucks, masters of the setting poles, the Creoles, famed far and wide as oarsmen, all the red-shirted band that dared the wrath of the river and paid its price? True, six of their peers had been hired as hands for the *New Orleans*— for such exciting duty as stoking fires!—but whether these watchers thought them fools or traitors or lucky men no one dared ask. The other spectators had their own opinions. Most of them considered the crew as well as the pilot and the engineer hardly less foolhardy than the Roosevelts themselves. And nobody could imagine how the two female servants and the waiter and the cook had been persuaded to go along, high wages or not. Perhaps it was their very lack of river experience that made them unafraid. Just fifteen people on a vessel designed with its spacious gentlemen's cabin and ample deck space, for seventy-five! The numbers told you there were not as many fools around as people thought. But if Mr. Roosevelt was ready to risk his life and his family's, too, why, who should quibble so long as the risks were not his own? The venture just might succeed, and if it did, the West would soon be trimming the sails of those eastern merchants, with their monopoly on trade. So ran the conversation on the shore that day.

Besides, just being there put one in a holiday mood. The Sunday clothes of the spectators were as bright as the reds and yellows of the autumn leaves that skipped and skittered down Boyd's Hill and along the riverbank. The southeast wind that teased them and promised more rain to swell the rivers—already most of the waiting flatboats at the Point had left, taking advantage of the flood—blew playfully too at the billowing black smoke and the sparks from the steamboat and pushed them toward town, where waste from cannon stoves and open grates, discharging into the streets, was drifting up to meet them. Across the turbid waters of the Monongahela, curling columns of smoke rose from Coal Hill, feeding the sullen pall that hung unendingly over the factories and coal pits to be turned by every errant townward breeze into a drizzle of soot that blackened roofs, seeped into shops and markets and churches, and darkened still more the once-white courthouse steeple that now appeared like an etching in charcoal against a hazy sky. Already Pittsburgh was the town where housewives cried to see their dirty curtains, and the snow was gray before it touched the ground.

But even the housewives saw silver in the sooty dust and gold in the snow. Pittsburgh was brimming with life, burgeoning, bursting at the seams. You could hear the sound of its growing in the rattle of immigrants' wagons on their way to the West, to Ohio, Kentucky, and Tennessee; in the bustle of shops supplying their needs and in the hawkers' cries in the streets; in the shouts of wagoners arriving with freight from Philadelphia in their red, white, and blue Conestogas, bells jingling as they rolled into town; in the gallop of hooves along cobblestoned streets and the accompanying cries of "Twenty-five dollars!" "Twenty-five dollars, fifty cents!" as a horse was auctioned on the run. You could hear it too in the hammer and whine and the roar of the factories and in the clink of the busy presses in Zadoc Cramer's printing shop or in the office of the *Pittsburgh Gazette* or in the babble of voices in the Diamond, the public square. The sound of the growing was unmistakable down at the Point, in the bump of barrels on cargo decks and the splash of oars; in the shouts of roistering keelers and the merry notes of the fiddle no boat would be without; in the lowing of cattle, the crowing of cocks, and the laughter and crying of children as family boats were loaded for the long float down the Ohio to Limestone and places beyond. And now it was loud in a brazen note new on the river, the triumphant roar of escaping steam, a sound that traveled on the wind toward the western waters, where before had been only the swish of oars and the hallooing voice of the boatman and the haunting call of his horn. And accompanying it, 22 the throb of laboring pistons, like the beat of a nation's pulse.

2

As a boy, Nicholas Roosevelt had seen the nation born. Only a stone's throw from his home, Israel Bissell on a Sunday noon in April of '75 galloped down Broadway shouting the news of Lexington. Over the same cobblestones, Lee and Schuyler and Washington passed on their momentous journey to Boston to assemble the troops. Washington, Nicholas remembered, was spendid in a dark blue uniform, with plumes in his hat, his carriage drawn by six white horses. He heard the stirring sound of militia marching on the common to the beat of the drum, watched in awe from his window as 130 ships of the British fleet whitened the harbor, exulted in the reflected glory of Roosevelt relatives in uniform—his brother James, just seventeen, serving without pay in the commissary of the Continental Army; his father, already blacklisted by the British as a Dutch malcontent, a private in Hay's Regiment; his cousin John, a captain in the blue and white of the Oswego Rangers; and, even more spectacularly, Cousin Nicholas wearing the red tin heart of "God and Right" on the green shirt of the Corsicans, with the motto "Liberty or Death" proclaimed on the crown of his round cocked hat. On the day that the troops assembled to hear the reading of the

Declaration of Independence, he saw the gilded statue of George III pulled down by the crowd on Bowling Green, that expanse of land that his grandfather and three others had rented from the city for one peppercorn a year in 1723 and made into what it was.

But he was to see little of the war.

When in mid-1776 it became clear that American prospects were dim and New York City would be a battleground, James Roosevelt, fifty-one and ready to fight, stripped his house as did everyone else of whatever could be melted into bullets—door knockers and sashweights and hinges, surely extra pain to a hardware man—and took his wife, Helena, Nicholas's stepmother, and younger children seventy-five miles upriver to the little town of Esopus (later Kingston). A town strongly Dutch from its beginnings, it had since the time of an earlier Nicholas been home to various Roosevelts; there any member of the clan—a large one by now, with fifty families in New York City alone—would be among friends. For seven years, while New York was a ghost city, with wharves crumbling and homes rotting and business at a standstill, with four hundred buildings in ruins from the great fire of 1776 and others converted into noisome prisons for the rebels, Nicholas went to school in Esopus and stayed safe with his three older sisters and two-year-old stepsister, Ann, in the comfortable home of a farmer named Joseph Oosterhaudt, about four miles out of town. The farm was far enough away to escape damage the following winter, when the British, angered by Revolutionary activity in Esopus, site of the state constitutional convention, burned it almost to the ground.

For the next six years, growing into the "burly farm boy" he would later remember as himself, Nicholas was free to follow paths that led away from the family hardware store, freer, perhaps, as a younger brother than he would have been were his place in the family different, the country not at war. His older brother James would on his discharge become the "Son" of Roosevelt & Son, the Maiden Lane firm that started the Oyster Bay branch of the Roosevelts on its prosperous way. Other Roosevelts, civic-minded and business-oriented, would follow the family pattern, taking seriously the family motto, "Qui Plantavit Curabit" (who planted it will care for it), investing their energies and funds in profitable pursuits, becoming aldermen and deacons and collectors of art, acquiring real estate in the tradition that had already made almost half of Manhattan Roosevelt ground, and engaging in conventional courtships, finding their spouses among other prominent New York families, the Barclays and the Schuylers, the Van Cortlands, the Van Nesses, and the Van Schaacks.

Not Nicholas. From the beginning he was a maverick, following his own bent. Born December 27, 1767, youngest of the eleven children of Jacobus I. Roosevelt by his first wife, Annetje Bogaert, he may have carried some of the nonconformist genes as well as the name of his great-grandfather Nicholas. It was great-grandfather Nicholas who amusedly defended his sprightly wife, Hillotje Jans, when her "luxurious petticoats" brought her to court on the charge of causing scandal. Unperturbed, her husband introduced a countercharge against the shocked town fathers, accusing them of slander. Or it may have been that the circumstances of the later Nicholas's early life shaped him in a different mold from that of his more conventional brothers. His mother died when he was only three, and until the birth of a daughter to his indulgent stepmother in 1775, he was the youngest of a large family and probably the freest to follow his fancies without pressure to conform.

Whatever the cause, he grew up asking different questions, getting different answers, not always the right ones. As an adult he showed neither the business nor the political sense that seemed bred in the genes of most Roosevelts; it was characteristic of him to embark on grandiose projects that more often than not sank beneath him, then to leap quite undismayed to the next. He distressed his friends with his irresponsibility and outraged his foes with his arrogance. He was devious enough to blame associates for his blunders and bold enough to face down an angry mob of Philadelphia citizens and a sheriff with a writ as they beat against the gates of the waterworks he was threatening to blow up.

Some of the questions he asked, even when very young,

were those being asked with increasing urgency in scattered parts of the world. New inventions in textile machinery and the development of the factory system were quickening the pace of industry, the pace of trade, hurrying the world along. The concept of automation and of interchangeable parts was about to transform the character of labor. The Industrial Revolution was burgeoning, and new clickety-clacking sounds, whirring sounds, the sounds of machinery, echoed from manufactories, troubling ears not yet attuned to a faster, noisier world. What makes things go? was the question asked. *What else might?*

Nicholas knew what made things go—water, wind, the muscle power of man or beast. Mills were a familiar part of his life. Wheat was ground on the New York waterfront; waterwheels powered his grandfather's linseed oil plant in Maiden Lane. When he walked north toward Minetta Brook to fish he saw windmills turning in the wind, water being drawn up for cattle, horses plodding patiently in an endless track to turn the grinding stones. He knew that the same forces, at odds, could make things not go—wind or water, a stubborn mule. He sat often on the stone wall that bordered the Hudson at the back of the Roosevelt land and watched ships sailing into New York harbor, following the struggles of the great square riggers as they fought the fierce north wind that barred them from safe anchorage. He dreamed then as humans had dreamed since Homer and before of "wondrous ships self-moved, instinct with mind," perhaps imagined magically powered oars or the harnessing of creatures of the sea.

Such visions as these, and the habit of observation, basic equipment for the inventor, traveled with him to Esopus. As he wandered the countryside, watching the blacksmith at his forge or chatting with the miller, hearing in the background the splashing sound of the waterwheel as it rose and fell, rose and fell, a nebulous wonder took on form and substance. He was interested in the emergence of metals from the earth, the shaping and balancing of them, what they could be made to do. His father was a gold- and silversmith as well as a merchant in hinges and plate glass and locks, and even at ten Nicholas had absorbed a good deal of knowledge about the potential of various metals.

Curious from the time he could remember, filled with the urge to tinker, to improve, he began during his years in Esopus to carry out "many actual experiments, as well upon mill machinery as upon the motion and buoyancy of bodies in and through the water; and . . ." (here, in an affidavit presented before the legislature of the state of New Jersey in 1814, he makes a significant claim), "did then and there make, rig, and put into operation, on a small brook near the house of the aforesaid Oosterhaudt, a small wooden boat or model of a boat with vertical wheels over the sides [and] these wheels being acted upon by hickory and whalebone springs propelled the model of the boat through the water by the agency of a tight cord passed between the wheels and being re-acted on by the springs."

Other testimony supports Roosevelt's claim that he conceived the idea of such paddle wheels long before Fulton's use of them. There are letters to and from Livingston and others, but he himself based his claim to priority on the performance of this little boat that made her maiden and only voyage on the Oosterhaudt brook. Long years after, on the basis of his affidavit, he was granted a patent, signed by President James Madison and Secretary of State James E. Monroe, that seems to acknowledge the validity of his claim, and on its merits received royalty rights. By then, hardly anyone cared.

Patent suits were far away, though, in those adolescent years, and when in 1783 James Roosevelt returned with his family to the Greenwich Street residence (it and the store both astonishingly undamaged by the fire and devastation that had destroyed so much of the city), Nicholas was still dreaming his dreams, tinkering with experiments that no one else in the family saw any sense in or cared about. The prospect of entering the hardware business filled him with dismay, and, as he was the youngest son and his brother James had already shown his aptitude for business, no great objection was made to his becoming a "mechanic" once his general education was complete. The now modest term then included metallurgist, machinist, even civil engineer—and enginemaker too, although no one in America had yet mastered that role.

As Nicholas started out, the sky looked bright, the horizon

limitless. Restrictions on trade with England during the Revolution had created a demand for domestic products, and a spirit of innovation and self-confidence stirred the inventive genius latent in the land. By 1790 the first Federal Patent Law would be enacted, one of its first patents going to Oliver Evans for an automatic grist mill; only two years later, Eli Whitney's cotton gin was to revolutionize the economy of the South. In post-Revolutionary New York, with a population approaching thirty thousand, demand for all manner of supplies and machinery was high. Nicholas was skillful, and he soon had smiths working under him. But even as he turned out the conventional wares—lathes and presses and clockwork machinery—he was distracted by reports of the work being done in Europe on engines powered by steam. Steam! Not water nor wind nor muscle, but a genie captured in a cylinder, in thrall to man. For a century it had been draining flooded mines, but grudgingly; now James Watt, in Edinburgh, had produced a revolutionary condensing engine that magically released that latent power. And the world as it was would be no more.

Nicholas was only one of many caught in the heady spell of new discovery in those days. The vistas opened by the power of steam were limitless. Distant horizons beckoned both actually and symbolically, for while horsepower and waterpower could turn the wheels adequately for many other purposes, their limits for transportation had been reached, and the world was in a hurry, the distances to be traveled greater than ever before.

That "fire-engines" might be used to move boats through water or carriages over land had occurred to many: as early as the thirteenth century Roger Bacon was suggesting that "chariots may be made so as to be moved with incalculable force, without any beast drawing them" and "engines of navigation . . . made without oarsmen." Thomas Savery, inventor of the fountain engine, suggested the possibility four centuries later, and in 1736 a Gloucestershire clockmaker named Jonathan Hulls patented a scheme for applying a Newcomen engine to a towboat by a system of weights and pulleys and strings and ratchets that was supposed to turn a single paddle wheel at the stern. Poor Jonathan

Hulls! He was so ridiculed for his ideas that he left his native village, where children chanted a ditty in his memory:

> *Jonathan Hulls*
> *With his patent skulls*
> *Invented a machine*
> *To go against wind and stream;*
> *But he, being an a--*
> *Couldn't bring it to pass,*
> *And so was ashamed to be seen.*

In France, the Marquis Claude de Jouffroy d'Abbans, who really did put a steamboat on the Saône River and moved it in the presence of thousands of people, including members of the Academy of Lyons, was just as effectively ridiculed, but by the savants of Paris. Called on to verify his success, the Academy of Sciences refused to accept the testimony of the provincial academicians, who, its members believed, could not possibly have seen what they said they saw. Jouffroy gave up, too.

Such experiments as these, though, were an ocean away and years earlier. It was when word trickled into New York late in August of 1787 that a steamboat had been made to travel at three miles an hour on the Delaware River, practically in his own backyard, that Nicholas really pricked up his ears. John Fitch, a wandering buttonmaker and self-taught silversmith, had propelled a boat by means of six paddles moving Indian style on either side so that it resembled a great water bug, showing it not only before jeering boatmen who delighted in racing past it but also before a number of delegates to the Constitutional Convention who happened to be at the site on their way to Philadelphia. Some of these delegates were favorably impressed and wrote laudatory letters to and about John Fitch, but General Washington and Dr. Franklin, among other influential men, had more faith in the work of James Rumsey, whose rivalry with Fitch was well known and who was, at least on the surface, a gentleman. Dr. Franklin particularly could not imagine that Fitch, a country bumpkin who looked like a scarecrow and acted like a boor, could produce *29*

anything worthwhile. Thenceforward, the American attitude toward John Fitch was set. Even later, when he had run a steamboat commercially along the Delaware on a regular schedule, and
later still, when Robert Fulton was reaping the fruits of the la-
bors of many men, Fitch continued in death as he had in life,
one of the least honored of American geniuses.

Nicholas, hearing the reports, remembered his little boat.
How splendid if he could try it now, full-size, with the magical
force of steam! But he was busy, busy; there was no time or money for experiments. At twenty-one, he was known as one of the
finest mechanics in the city. In 1791, when he was twenty-four,
he had the foresight and either the funds or credit to join his
brother John in the purchase of 500,000 acres of land in Oswego
County, in upstate New York, paying three shillings and one
pence per acre. Two years later, he became director of the New
Jersey Copper Mine Association organized to rework the abandoned Schuyler copper mine at North Arlington, New Jersey,
and the following year bought the lease on the mines, then for
sale. Now he was acting like a Roosevelt! Even the most critical
of his relatives, and evidently they were critical, must have been
impressed, but not sufficiently so to put their names on the mortgage. The names that did appear on it were those of his good
friends Jacob and Rosetta Mark, who were to play a key role in
the lives of Nicholas and Lydia, and of John and Catherine
Speyer.

Enthusiastic, ebullient, determined to build engines to rival
England's, Roosevelt erected above the mine a metal foundry and
machine shop patterned after the famous Boulton and Watts
works, naming it the American Soho Works after its English
counterpart. Here was built the first steam engine made in
America. In company with Mark, he applied unsuccessfully for
a monopoly on copper mining and prospecting in the United
States, an attempt he took care not to mention in Pittsburgh.
He took in as a partner James Smallman, formerly of the Boulton
factory, with whom he invented and patented a double-acting engine, and on a gentle rise overlooking the Passaic River built a
gracious country home, which he called Laurel Hill. At thirty,

recognized as the only enginebuilder of consequence in America, Nicholas Roosevelt was not only on his way, he was already there.

What happened?

After that peak of promise, his career plummeted, and whether his fortunes, or lack of them, were of his own making is a tantalizing question. But then, so are most of the questions about him.

Early in his career two disastrous debacles followed what should have been profitable investments and plunged him into enormous debt. In carrying out a contract for supplying spikes and bolts to the Navy in 1798, Roosevelt hired sub-contractors who used base metal. The products were rejected. His attempts to prosecute the coppermining company were unsuccessful, passing the House but being defeated in the Senate by the single vote of Gouverneur Morris. While this suit was pending, he received another potentially valuable contract. The Federalist Congress, under President John Adams, who was a big-Navy man and favored a strong fleet, authorized the building of six seventy-four-gun frigates in preparation for a possible war with France. The contract for copper sheathing for the hulls went to Roosevelt. Elated, he undertook the construction of the rolling mill needed, expanded facilities, employed more workmen, and set about obtaining the copper, all the while, in accordance with the terms of the contract, borrowing large sums against his notes. Alas, politics soon reared its treacherous head. (Nicholas Roosevelt would never have any head for it at all.) With the inauguration of Jefferson, the pro-French party came into power. France was the darling of the administration, and the prospect of war, at least with France, became unthinkable. The order for the frigates was cancelled. Too bad for Mr. Roosevelt! No payment to him was ever made; he was sued for the money borrowed, and for years thereafter he was in the Navy's debt, underfinanced and skittering on the edge of ruin.

Overlapping this disaster came the fiasco of his two years' collaboration with Robert Livingston in the building of a steamboat. Excited by the prospect of having a long-dreamed-of project financed, flattered by association with one of the wealthiest and most powerful men in America, and believing that he could persuade Livingston of the greater feasibility of paddle wheels over Livingston's own impractical plan for a submerged box with an elaborate pump system, Roosevelt devoted two years, enormous energy, and large sums of money, again borrowed, in a vain effort to accomplish his dream. The experience was harrowing. Livingston, used to playing important political and social roles, was an arrogant man who fancied himself a great inventor. He treated Roosevelt, despite a nominal partnership, as simply a hired hand. On a sudden notion he would order a part taken out, a part added; he would order alterations that required complete rebuilding and a week later demand that the laggard workmen be fired. All failures were ascribed to the engine, never to the Livingston design. And of course Roosevelt was spending too much money. (How familiar this criticism would become!) As to Roosevelt's initially hopeful and tentative, then bold, and finally desperate suggestions—in 1798, remember, years before the *Clermont*—that wheels over the side be tried, they were, pronounced the great inventor, "out of the question."

Livingston is the villain here, politics and the dishonesty of others in the earlier disasters. But Roosevelt was more often his own villain. He speculated unwisely and recklessly in land and minerals and acted irresponsibly, even shamefully, toward his associates. Benjamin Latrobe, who in the first flush of friendship endorsed the Navy notes, was allowed for years to bear the brunt of the indebtedness, throwing precious sums he could ill afford at the creditors who nipped at Roosevelt's nimble heels. And yet, such ambivalence could Roosevelt arouse in others that even Latrobe, at the same time that he labeled Roosevelt "a most inveterate schemer [who] lives as naturally in scrapes, as a salamander does in the fire," could praise his "kind heart" and "natural and principled honesty." A descendant Nicholas Roosevelt, journalist and diplomat, rationalized his relative's failures as due to a lack of "the acquisitive instinct so strong in others of his tribe [by which] he might have become a powerful figure in the industrialization of America."

A kind excuse, but hardly convincing. For Roosevelt was no dreamy inventor, gently brushing off thoughts of gain. He always *intended* success—and a profit. His was a complex character, that of a vital, even boisterous man, unpredictable, stubborn, and exasperating, but clearly blessed with some paradoxical charm. He retained the affection of friends even as he tried them sorely. He was esteemed by his peers despite awkward and public financial embarrassments. He won the complete and enduring love of a beautiful, popular girl half his age who was courted by suitors far more eligible. And he seems in retrospect totally appealing even as he flouts convention and good sense.

Certainly he appealed to Lydia Latrobe.

She was ten when they met, thirteen when he proposed, seventeen when, after a courtship partly Shakespeare, partly farce, they were married. And lived happpily ever after, for years and years and years.

Had Philadelphia not wanted a new water system, the two might never have met.

Benjamin Henry Latrobe visited the Soho Works in the fall of 1798 to confer with Roosevelt about the building of two enormous pumps for the Philadelphia waterworks, which he had been commissioned to design. At the time, Roosevelt was becoming discouraged with the progress of the steamboat project on which he was working with Livingston. Latrobe, an English architect who had migrated to Virginia two years earlier following the death of his wife and who had left behind with his sisters his small son and daughter, was becoming discouraged about the laggard pace of his professional career. Architecture was not highly regarded in the utilitarian climate of America, where it seemed fancy nonsense to pay someone to draw pictures of a house when members of the carpenters' companies would throw in the design with the cost of building. Latrobe had been awarded the waterworks commission in his capacity as an engineer, and then only after a long battle against hostile political forces.

It happens occasionally that two personalities are instantly compatible. So it was with these two men. Both ambitious, both with great plans and bold ones but without resources for carrying them out, familiar with the frustrations of being thwarted by moneyed philistines, both young and eager (Roosevelt was thirty-one, Latrobe thirty-four), they became close friends almost at once. Their personalities must have been remarkably complementary, for they were certainly not alike. Latrobe was highly educated, an accomplished musician, artist, and linguist. He knew seven languages. His interests were diverse; politics, biology, and literature alike were grist for speculation. He was an emotional man who suffered often from depression. Roosevelt was like the country—pragmatic, venturesome, optimistic, turbulent in nature, not especially interested in politics or in cultural concerns but enormously curious about *things*. Nonetheless, in each other they found a reflection of their own dreams and best self-images. Roosevelt's faith in the future of steam, his confidence that American copper would soon take precedence over English, Latrobe's visions of beautiful buildings, his dreams for the future of architecture in America—all sorts of ideas crowded the minds of both of them (a bridge to connect New York City with Long Island across Blackwell's Island, for instance—that was Roosevelt's). There was so much to share under the bright October sky! They agreed that the lot of the innovator was a sorry one. When Latrobe related his struggles to have his ideas for the waterworks project accepted, Roosevelt was indignant. When he told of the skepticism expressed by some committee members and editorially by the *Philadelphia Gazette* about the wisdom of investing in steam engines, "machines of all machinery the least to be relied on, subject to casualties and accidents of every kind," Roosevelt was incensed. Here indeed was a challenge to the foremost builder of steam engines in America! He himself, he declared, would collaborate with Latrobe on the project and together they would get that waterworks built and make the Philadelphians eat—or drink—their words.

So great was the rapport at that first meeting, or so great the Roosevelt charm, deliberately exerted or not, that by the time it was over, Latrobe, who held as security some land in Pennsylvania inherited from his mother, had endorsed the Navy notes. Later, when the city of Philadelphia, not so easily captivated, demanded some surety that Roosevelt would not default on the engine contract, through negligence or the engine's inadequacy, Roosevelt mortgaged his engine works to the city as security. Now the futures of both of them were hostage, and entangled in the first strands of what would become an unbreakable web.

Latrobe was then already courting Mary Elizabeth Hazlehurst, the lovely and talented daughter of a prominent Philadelphia family. The wedding, almost as fateful for Roosevelt as for the principals, took place in May of 1800. During the preceding months Latrobe had kept in close touch with Roosevelt, and it was with special delight that he brought his bride, while on their wedding trip, to Laurel Hill to meet his closest friend. Mary Elizabeth, like her husband, felt toward Roosevelt the warm affection he seemed to inspire so effortlessly and joined Latrobe in urging upon him a standing invitation to visit them in Philadelphia. The newlyweds had another invitation to issue immediately upon their return home, one that Mary Elizabeth had made a condition of their marriage: Latrobe sent at once for his two children, Lydia, nine, and Henry, eight, whom he had missed grievously. And it was not long after the children's arrival, in the autumn of 1800, that Nicholas Roosevelt traveled to Philadelphia to be welcomed and made much of and to be accepted at once by the children as "Uncle Nick." And to return. And return. And return.

How soon Roosevelt realized that he was in love we do not know; he told Lydia by the time she was twelve. And look askance as we may at so disparate a romance, true love it manifestly was. Perhaps he could not at first admit even to himself that this pretty, dark-haired child, lively and bright, with a grave maturity, had captured his heart as no woman had so far been able to do. He knew only that his visits to the Latrobes were the highlight of his life and that, close as he felt to them all, it was when Lydia came into a room that the sunshine came too. Certainly it did not occur to Lydia's father or to Mary Elizabeth that their good friend's affection for the children was other than

35

avuncular, and they extended toward him an unfailing warmth of welcome that drew him into the family circle. At 186 Arch Street in Philadelphia and later at Newcastle, Delaware, where they moved when Latrobe was surveying the route for the Chesapeake and Delaware Canal, and then at Iron Hill, near Elkton in Maryland, Roosevelt was a frequent visitor. And when, in the autumn of 1803, twelve-year-old Lydia was sent to school at Jaudon's Academy, solicitous Uncle Nick managed to find his way there. A thoughtful family friend, indeed, much cherished. Even when his irresponsibility as a business partner became apparent and the Navy debt an albatross to Latrobe, even when, naively or otherwise, Nicholas shifted the blame from himself to Latrobe for delays in the waterworks project, Latrobe could still declare, "if there is anything certain under heaven, it is that you hold the first place in our esteem, good opinion & friendship."

And all the while . . .

That was the incredible part! That, all the while, Roosevelt had been courting Lydia; for when he approached the stunned parents in the autumn of 1804 with a declaration of his love for her, they learned that Lydia was not stunned at all. Yes, she was in love with Uncle Nick, she assured them complacently. And he with her. And everything was settled between them.

To Latrobe the shock was enormous. Roosevelt was his closest friend, his business partner, his *contemporary*. Lydia was his child, his firstborn, and especially dear. She was a girl exceptionally gifted, educated beyond contemporary female standards, imbued with the high artistic and intellectual values of two brilliant and loving parents (for her stepmother had taken the two children completely into her heart), astonishingly capable and kind in her care of her stepsiblings, "the little folk," as their father called them. Mature for her years, but still—a child! Latrobe could summon only one defense—laughter.

"Were you really serious?" he wrote in light tone to Roosevelt, who was by then back in Philadelphia. Oh, come on, my friend. . . .

In answer Roosevelt wrote not to him but to Mary Elizabeth, believing her more understanding. Yes, he was very serious.

Latrobe was dismayed, angry. He had other troubles that were driving him to distraction: riots among his laborers, Federalist attacks on him in the newspapers, troubles with creditors. And now this. The idea was preposterous!

"On the subject on which you have written Mrs. L.," he wrote, "we had better *talk* than *write*. Perhaps it will be still better to *laugh*."

Poor father. There was to be no laughter. Instead, confrontation, pleas, arguments, questions. How could a beloved family friend so take advantage of his welcome? How would a financially unstable, mercurial, gifted but unpredictable mechanical engineer support a wife? And so young a wife! Did Nicholas really believe that a child's fondness could be interpreted as the love of a mature woman? Clearly he did. Appeals to Lydia's usual good sense got nowhere, and by mid-December Latrobe had agreed to meet Roosevelt in Philadelphia over Christmas to "talk." Three months later, so persistent was Roosevelt, so determined Lydia, and so genuine the affection that the Latrobes felt for this maddening, impossible, crisis-causing "dear friend" that on Lydia's fourteenth birthday, Nicholas Roosevelt, having drawn the teeth of Latrobe's material objections by a proposed settlement on his bride of twenty thousand dollars worth of real estate, was accepted as Lydia's unannounced fiancé. Upon this "grand event," her father lamented, his daughter became "silent, & as affected as a Cat. I don't know what to do with her. . . ."

What he did was to seize time as an ally, imposing a year's probation as the condition for his consent to the marriage. During that time there was to be no pleading for an earlier union, no private meetings, no clandestine correspondence. Ah, Montagues and Capulets! Impatient with the delay, as head over heels in love as a moonstruck boy, Roosevelt violated the moratorium almost at once. He secretly sent letters suggesting elopement and urging Lydia to marry him at once. Worse still, he managed private meetings when he knew the Latrobes were absent from home, thereby arousing Latrobe's first real anger against his friend.

And then what Latrobe must have considered a miracle took place. The wedding was scheduled for Lydia's fifteenth birthday, 37

March 23, 1806, and Latrobe, resigned, had written to his brother in England requesting a copy of Lydia's birth certificate and a settlement of her mother's estate so that she might receive her inheritance. (She never did.) Roosevelt had been making frequent visits, and Mary Elizabeth and Lydia were excitedly making wedding plans. Between visits, Lydia and Roosevelt had been carrying on a correspondence under the conditions imposed by Latrobe, and Lydia, with an openness that touched her parents' hearts, showed them her letters to Roosevelt and often his to her. The courtship was progressing smoothly; peace had been established between the father of the bride and his son-in-law to be.

Suddenly, there was a quarrel, an apparently irrevocable quarrel. Lydia refused even to answer Roosevelt's letters and announced decisively that there would be no wedding. And only then did her father learn of the deception that had been carried on for over a year. Lydia had indeed been showing them her letters and Roosevelt's, but they were not the letters that mattered. At Roosevelt's suggestion ("you have taught my child deceit," cried Latrobe), others had been secretly exchanged and—a revelation learned humiliatingly from Jacob Mark in New York— an elopement had actually been planned.

It was too much. Their business association could not easily be dissolved, but for months thereafter whatever exchange of letters was necessary between the two men showed Latrobe coldly angry and Roosevelt at first bitter, even to the point of insult. Then—well, he was what he was, and there were so many other things to think about, such as the new and ingenious uses of steam power. Oliver Evans, whose reputation as a builder of engines was pressing Roosevelt's uncomfortably, had erected a steam-powered dredging machine on a small scow to which wheels could be attached. He had actually run it around Centre Square in Philadelphia and then lumbered on into the Schuylkill, where it was used to clear the channel. There was also the steamboat that Livingston and Fulton were building at Paulus Hook, similar to one they had tried out on the Seine a year or so earlier. It was to be 133 feet long, with a thirty-foot stack, machinery exposed amidships, and side paddle wheels. Side paddle wheels!

That Livingston was now collaborating with Fulton on what had originally been Roosevelt's proposal rankled, as it always would; but with a shrug Nicholas turned to other things. He had managed to wriggle out of debt on the waterworks project in connection with a syndicate, as Latrobe had not; now he invested in salt meadowlands in New Jersey and associated Latrobe with him in the purchase without obligation. He also set about reestablishing his enginebuilding business. Within a year, he was involved in a number of promising projects and the two men were friends again. After all, the ridiculous romance was safely over, wasn't it? And Lydia was sixteen now, more mature.

Besides, the family was moving to Washington City, where Latrobe was to redesign the President's House. In that raw, smelly Federal city, with its short rows of brick houses rising from vacant land, its drab boardinghouses crowded with congressmen whose wives would not bring their children to this malarial town, its stinking canal that would one day be Constitution Avenue but into which butchers now tossed offal, its clouds of flies swarming from private stables and cow barns, its rutted streets—with all that, there was a heady excitement and a round of activities and a delightful surplus of men that would distract any girl from old loves. Here ambassadors in exotic garb and Indian chiefs and men in small clothes with gold knee buckles and women in satin and lace mingled at the President's balls. At the race track (Congress adjourned for the races), the President and other privileged spectators cantered about while ladies like Mrs. Madison, wife of the secretary of state, and Mrs. Gallatin, wife of the treasury secretary, and Mrs. Van Ness from New York looked on from carriages nearby. And in Washington the Latrobes had social and political ties that would insure their inclusion in the glittering social life of the capital.

The Latrobe home, in fact, became something of a salon, noted for the sparkling tenor of the conversation and the impressive credentials of the guests. The James Madisons came, and the Henry Clays and the Albert Gallatins, Chief Justice Marshall, the Russian minister Dashkoff and his American wife, others equally interesting, and—because Lydia was one of the most attractive

Lydia Latrobe Roosevelt. From a portrait
in the possession of the Nicholas Latrobe
Roosevelts. By permission of William
Morrow Roosevelt.

girls in Washington—a number of young men not terribly concerned even with hearing Mrs. Latrobe's beautiful singing voice
or in taking part in the always stimulating discussions. Lieuten-
ant Brooks, one of the handsomest men in the Navy, was a frequent visitor (he would die on the deck of the *Lawrence*); Captain
David Porter, later commodore, was one of Lydia's most impor-
tunate suitors and the one most favored by her father; young men
from the diplomatic corps were especially pleased to be invited
to a Latrobe evening. Lydia received them all. She danced and

partied, turned down proposals with light laughter, and when Nicholas Roosevelt came to call one September day in 1808 her decision was made in an hour. There could never have been any other.

They were married at home on Tuesday evening, the fifteenth of November 1808, by the Reverend Mr. McCormick. Lydia was seventeen, Roosevelt forty-one. He arrived on the preceding Sunday in his own carriage (bought for the occasion), bringing with him Lydia's brother Henry from St. Mary's Academy in Baltimore and looking, Lydia thought, wonderfully handsome in his morning clothes, with that interesting touch of gray in his blond hair and the crinkles around his blue eyes. How dull, how young, how unexciting all those others were! Only a few friends were invited to the wedding, but among them Dolley Madison was an especially welcome guest; it was she who had most convinced the anxious father that a difference in age should be no bar to happiness. After all, her "Jemmy" was almost twenty years older than she (and homely besides!).

But was she right? Benjamin Latrobe, holding his almost fainting daughter in his arms the next morning, seeing her tears as she bade her family goodbye, supporting her as she made her way to the carriage, wondered. As do we. Was Nicholas showing rare understanding in allowing his wife's father those few moments of closeness? Or was he so annoyed by Lydia's emotionalism—what did it say for the wedding night, after all!—that he simply stood aside during this evidently painful scene? We have only Latrobe's account. No matter. With whatever sadness on Lydia's part, with whatever relief on her husband's (one suspects it was great), they were soon on their way to New York and a home with Jacob and Rosetta Mark, with whom Nicholas always stayed in New York and whose importance in the Roosevelts' lives Latrobe would always resent.

A year earlier, in August of 1807, a strange, dark-looking craft, propelled by side paddle wheels, Robert Fulton's *North River Steamboat of Clermont,* had made her successful debut on the Hudson.

A year later, in 1809, at the earnest request of Latrobe, who 41 was seeking desperately some way to set his son-in-law on a hopeful course, Roosevelt became a partner in the Mississippi Steamboat Navigation Company. In a springless coach—no springs could last on the rocking, dragging journey across ravines and gullies and chasms, up and down steep precipices for which tree trunks had to be attached to the coach as drags—he and Lydia set off over the mountains for Pittsburgh and their rendezvous with the rivers of the West.

3

The winds blew from the southwest.

They pushed at the black smoke that belched into the pure, clean air, worried it, urged it back toward the East, away from this virgin sky. The smoke, sooty and thick, broke, dissolved, re-formed, swelled, drifted across the water and over the bluffs serene in their curtains of trees, dropped its murky residue on giant red and golden sycamores, on great, hanging grapevines now autumn-bare, on beeches, oaks, black willow. A few sparks fell.

Andrew Jack, the pilot of the *New Orleans,* feeling the steady vibration of the engine, the regular movement of beam and piston, noting their speed—eight to ten miles an hour—delighting in the wheel's eager response to his touch, nodded approvingly. This first day out she'd come through the roaring chute of Dead Man's Riffle with barely a shudder, skirted the hazardous tips of islands invisible at high water, maneuvered her way through narrow, winding channels. Oh, he'd had misgivings, all right; he'd be the first to admit it. But Mr. Roosevelt knew what he was doing; the steamboat was fine as silk.

And how she brought the people running! A man could 43

hardly help preening a little, laughing almost, to see them staring and pointing, some of them so frightened they stayed hiding in the woods while the *New Orleans* went speeding by. They came from cabins hidden among the trees or appeared on the crests of the forested hills; at tiny settlements they watched from fields dotted with burned-out stumps. And always there were children, children by the dozens, spilling out ahead. At Beaver, surely the whole town had left houses and shops and inns and even Mr. Grier's new brewery to stand on the bluff high above the river and wave and shout. Soon they would be passing Steubenville. There was a bad riffle there, with the channel well to the right. Andrew Jack's memory bank was stored with such data for instant retrieval, his pilot's brain programmed to respond to the faintest dimple in the water that warned of a rock or a wreck, to the long, slanting line that showed a bluff reef and to the fringe that marked its head, to the lines and circles in slick water made by a developing shoal, to every changing shape and shadow that warned of danger or showed the way. Driftwood told him a story; so did the lean of a tree and the level of the sediment that clung to the bank. At Wheeling, according to orders, they would round to. Something about letters to mail, and a plan Mr. Roosevelt had for the steamboat to earn a little profit along the way.

The pilot glanced back toward the stern deck, where Mr. and Mrs. Roosevelt stood talking to Baker, the engineer. The big dog, Tiger, stood beside them, facing the wind so that it ruffled his silky black fur. The little girl, he supposed, was taking her afternoon nap in the ladies' cabin, where from the looks of her mother she'd soon have a brother or sister to help keep the two maids hopping. The younger one wouldn't have so much time then to toss her pretty head at Baker, blushing the way she did at his teasing. If Jack agreed privately with those who thought Mrs. Roosevelt should have stayed on the solid ground of Pittsburgh, he shrugged the thought away. Guiding the vessel skillfully around Neasley's Cluster and the snag that marked the channel to the left of Tumbleton's Island, he was concerned with matters more immediate.

Mrs. Roosevelt herself appeared not to be worried at all, just excited, pointing toward one of the islands ahead, where a family of cranes, part of the lush, exuberant life of the rich riverlands, walked about on stiltlike legs. Earlier, they had seen a peregrine falcon drop fierce and deadly on its prey, one of a great V of ducks high in the air, and snow geese had passed, too, on their way south. From a nearby point, three solemn pelicans took measured flight, and for an instant a flash of silver broke the surface of the water, token of the teeming, busy company beneath, the hosts of perch and herring and sturgeon and pike and enormous catfish that could people a fisherman's dreams. On this, along this, in and above this "Belle Riviere," this ancient river more ancient than the greater stream toward which it flowed, creation flourished. In the heavily timbered forests, where sycamores grew to such a size that thirteen men on horseback had been known to stand in the hollow of one, with room for more, where grapevines hung spreading canopies sixty to eighty feet above the ground, where the high bluffs and low bottomlands, alternating in elegant balance, divided among themselves an infinite variety of trees—oak and hickory and ash and chestnut, maple and locust, tulip and black willow—a thousand, thousand creatures walked and crawled and flew and scurried. Wild turkeys and pheasants and partridges stirred the grasses, bright green parakeets wheeled in clouds, robins and grackles and orioles and ivory-billed woodpeckers sang and trilled and tapped. Pronghorned deer, alert only to the old familiar dangers, turned soft brown eyes on passing boats, while deep in the woods their enemies stalked, bears and panthers and wolves. Out on the river, wild geese skimmed the water; ducks unnumbered—teal and ring-necked, pintail and golden-eye—flew and settled; whooping cranes walked on the sandbars where sometimes a swan set down, preening its feathers. Here and there an eagle plummeted to seize in cruel claws a careless carp and rise gloriously to the sky. The settlements of man were still timid encroachments, intrusions not yet able to change the character of this land, the river's land.

Four to six hundred yards across, widening to a thousand and more at the Falls of the Ohio, the river unfurled in bends

45

about a mile long, and finely improved by its proprietor, doctor Brunot, well known for his hospitality to strangers and friends, and his taste in horticulture.

Irwin's (now Neville's) island, No. 2, three miles below No. 1,   4 | 6

At the head of this island, is a bar putting out towards the right shore, therefore you must keep about one-third of the river to your right, and at the *first ripple*, opposite Baldwin's stone mill, leave a breaker or rock a little to your right. Thence bear towards the island, to avoid the second, *or Horse-tail ripple*, which is about half way down the island, leaving a bar to the right, and some breakers to the left.

No. 2 is a fine large island, about six miles long, possessing several good farms and other improvements. It belongs to the family of general Neville of Pittsburgh.

Hog island, No. 3, just below and joined to No. 2 by a bar.

This island, though very small, forms a considerable impediment to this part of the river. The channel is uncommonly crooked, narrow, and difficult to hit, hence, the greater care is required. At its head a bar extends out, and obliges you to keep pretty close to the right shore, thence pull for the island, keeping pretty close to it, and take the chute which runs directly across to the left shore towards Middletown, and close under the foot of the island, leaving a broad flat bar to your right, on the head of which there is a danger of grounding, without great care inspection, and hard pulling or poling, for there is a great proportion of the river runs over this bar, but not a sufficient depth to afford a boat channel, unless in a rise of the river, notwithstanding a channel through the bar has been attempted by artificial means, running in a direct line with the river above.

After you get through the Hog island chute and floating near the left shore a short distance, the channel bears to the right considerably, and at the distance of half or three quarters of a mile below Hog island, having about two-thirds of the river to your left, you pass the *Third or Hosiery's ripple, or trap.*

Dead-man's island, No. 4, and ripple,   9 | 15

This is a very small island, and in floods nothing is seen of it but the willows growing on it. The channel is somewhat difficult and serpentine in very low stages of the water. A bar extends upwards from the head of the island, which forms a ripple, and which you avoid by pulling for the right shore as soon as you get near it, leaving the head of the bar and island to the left. After this first chute to the right, bear towards the island,

Specimen pages from Zadok Cramer's *The Navigator,* edition of 1814.

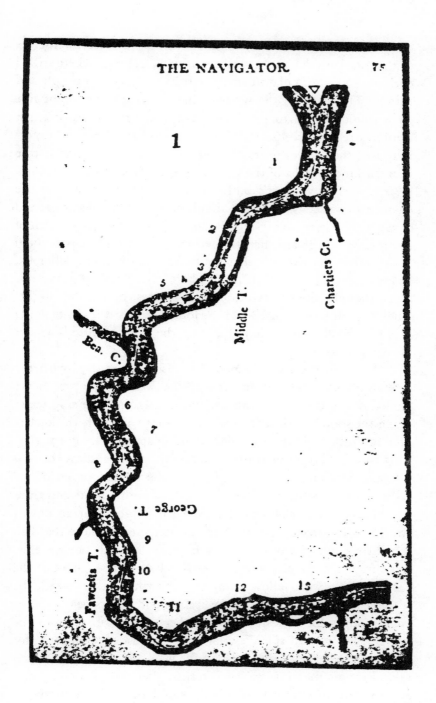

and curves and sudden reaches, in twists that reversed themselves so that head winds caught vessels unaware, in bends where stilled currents and eddies played with the floating freight of people and things. The errancy, the whims, that spurned the straight line gave scenic beauty to its thousand-mile course, toward which minion streams, creeks, and rivers large and small hurried eagerly to lose themselves in its broader stream. Along its course rose islands, ninety-eight of them according to Zadoc Cramer's *Navigator,* the river voyager's bible, from which they learned of the channel's course, the hazards ahead, and the best places to land or embark. These ninety-eight islands gave to the river much of its beauty and greater hardship to the pilot's task. Upon them it deposited the rich silt that made fruits grow more delicious, larger, more abundant than anywhere else, or so it was said. Some thought the river's beauty was greatest on autumn nights when the whitecaps tossed and the forests were silvered where the rays of a bright moon played among the peeled white branches of the sycamores.

Now, in the late afternoon of this October day, with the river high and the current strong, the *New Orleans* was never alone. A few upward-bound keelboats, hugging the easy water along the shore, worked their way laboriously upriver, the keelers bending into their setting poles, walking stooped along the running boards, returning swiftly in an ever-moving endless chain— Lift and Set! Lift and Set! But by far the larger burden of the river was the parade of arks and barges, of family boats and trading boats, and of keelboats loaded with freight floating downward on the current or rowing for greater speed. Those that had left Pittsburgh that day had long been left behind, but travelers fresh from a night's stay at Beaver Creek or Grape Island or the Little Yellow were fellow voyagers for a time; others would be gliding into the procession at Wheeling and points below. Some were heading for Limestone, Ohio, there to disembark and journey by land toward the West; others were loaded with cargo for New Orleans or settlements along the way. Were the *New Orleans* one of them, meeting on equal terms, the crews hallooing and the fiddlers sharing a tune, there would be the customary exchange of questions: "Where're you bound?" "What's your lading?" "Who's your captain?" and farther on, when many had passed and parted and others come, the familiar "Where're you from?" But now, high above ordinary people in ordinary vessels, attracting stares and creating consternation, enveloped in the sound of laboring piston and rumbling boiler and the slap and splash of wheels, the steamboat's crew could only shout a few rivermen's insults, hear above the throb of the engine a few notes of the fiddler's song or the sound of a horn, and wave as they pulled abreast and then quickly past, with the tunes of the fiddle still dancing in their heads:

> *The boatman is a lucky man,*
> *No one can do as the boatman can,*
> *The boatmen dance and the boatmen sing,*
> *The boatman is up to everything.*
>
> *Hi-O, away we go,*
> *Floating down the river on the O-hi-o.*

"Here she comes!"

Wheeling was a-buzz and a-bustle with anticipation. The word had traveled along the river, carried by flatboat and barge; it had come in with Wheelingites back from the fifty-eight-mile journey by horseback to Pittsburgh, some of them businessmen who had seen the *New Orleans* on the ways. It had traveled out, too, to inland villages and towns, by way of the mail coach that racketed twice weekly into town from Philadelphia and Baltimore. It was spread by the posters sent out by that indefatigable promoter Nicholas Roosevelt telling of the "Modern Marine Curiosity" that would be open to inspection during its stay at Wheeling for a fee—most reasonable, surely—of twenty-five cents.

This day the mouth of Wheeling Creek, a popular place for embarkation downriver, was crowded with vessels delaying departure, and along the narrow top of Wheeling Creek Hill wag- 49 ons from as far away as Washington, Pennsylvania, came lumbering single file. Townspeople hurried along the populous single street, three-quarters of a mile long, that was squeezed between the river and the hill's high, steep sides and gathered on the bottom below the town, where the warehouse and rope walk and boatyard were located and where Sprigg's tavern was jammed now and alive with the movement of customers and the buzz of talk and the pungent whisky smell. Those who remembered reminded one another of the Roosevelts' earlier visit, in the flatboat. It was a very elegant one, people remarked. Mrs. Roosevelt was said to have designed the interior herself, with its comfortable bedroom, dining room, and pantry, and a room forward for the crew, with a fireplace where the cooking was done. On the flat top of the boat were seats and an awning, very fancy. Such work seemed an unlikely job for a woman, but then Mrs. Roosevelt was an unlikely woman, when you got right down to it. Most Wheelingites, like many other people in many other places, were not quite sure whether they approved or disapproved of her, but they did wonder about her good sense. It hadn't seemed reasonable then that any woman, unless she was part of a family of settlers moving on, would undertake so arduous and lengthy a voyage for no reason, especially when she would be likely confined before the trip was done. (Oh, yes, you can take our word for it! the sharp-eyed women had said.) And when they had been told by the Roosevelts themselves about their plans for the steamboat, a vessel with *wheels* (on a boat!) and a fire engine to make them move, there had been some with gumption enough to tell them to their faces that they were as looney as a slooney with the peedoodles.

It hadn't fazed them one bit. The pilot told those who asked that Mr. Roosevelt was on his way to make a survey of the rivers, of every island and ripple and snag, and to measure currents and chart channels, for even Zadoc Cramer's *Navigator* did not show where the channels were wide and deep enough for a vessel with a seven-foot hull (which turned out to be a twelve-foot one). He was on his way to pick out landing places and see where wood could best be taken on for burning and maybe even coal as well, although below Grave Creek, just past Wheeling, there was little sign of any. It was interesting that on that earlier voyage Mr. Roosevelt was guiding himself by the *Navigator* and now he was in it himself. Zadoc Cramer had seen the steamboat on the stocks and hurried to take notice of "A Mr. Rosewalt, a gentleman of enterprize," and his exciting plan that, "if it succeeds, must open to view flattering prospects to an immense country. . . ." "It will be a novel sight," he'd said, "and as pleasing as novel, to see a huge boat working her way up the windings of the Ohio without the appearance of sail, oar, pole or any manual labor about her— moving within the secrets of her own wonderful mechanism, and propelled by power undiscoverable."

It would be indeed! But that such a sight would ever be seen seemed as unlikely to people in Wheeling as to sensible people anywhere else in the West. Even if the skeptics had now been proved wrong—the boat was here, you couldn't get around that—they still maintained that they were half right. She hadn't come up, had she? *That's* what they wanted to see!

Even the skeptics, though, had to inspect this great wonder; for one thing, a person would be left out afterward if he couldn't talk about the steamboat and how she looked and sounded and what he thought her chances were. There were few who did not join the procession (and even they came out to look) that wound down to the landing and up the plank put out for boarding, pay- ing their twenty-five cents as they came aboard. They glanced curiously at the great chimney that rose smack in the middle of the vessel and that looked somehow clumsy and wrong compared to the two slender masts that stood fore and aft and the graceful eight-foot-long bowsprit with its carved figurehead. Mr. Roose- velt himself pointed out the marvels of the machinery amidships, telling some of the visitors more than they really wanted to know or could even make any sense of. Only a few cared that the engine was a low-pressure one, with a thirty-four-inch cylinder, its in- terior hand filed, or quite understood just how power traveled from the firebox to the boiler to the piston to the beam, but they did inspect with more than passing interest the paddle wheels, which made the vessel look like a floating sawmill coming down   *51* the river. The arms, they saw, were of wood, and the attached floats, or paddles, of sheet iron, so adjusted by screws and holes, as Mr. Roosevelt explained, that they could dig deeper in water or less so according to the draft of the vessel or her burden. Clever.

Most of the visitors were more eager to see the cabins they had heard described as so elegant. Allowed to look in, they saw that there were two, actually one cabin divided, the ladies' cabin aft and the gentlemen's forward, the two separated by a folding door. The first and smaller one, the ladies', held four berths and was comfortably furnished, with damask hangings around the berths and looking glasses against the walls and an elegant carpet on the floor. High windows along the side gave a light and airy appearance to what could have been a dismal setting, situated as the cabin was in the hold. The much larger forward cabin, with a greater number of berths, set in tiers along either side and having curtains to shield them from public view, was to be reserved for gentlemen, although now the only "gentleman" aboard was Mr. Roosevelt himself, who evidently occupied the aft cabin with his wife. In the center of this cabin was a long table for dining— as on later steamboats, the ladies would join the gentlemen at mealtimes, but only then. There was no carpet. As it would throughout the steamboat era, prudence dictated that the floor of the gentlemen's cabin remain bare. Tobacco stained. Comfortable chairs were set up along the sides, however, and in the forward area was a stove for heating, with wood stacked in a neat pile beside it. A leather firebucket stood handily by. Shelves along the walls held dishes and what anybody could see was a collection of fine wines. Cooking was done in a galley forward, where a huge wood stove had space for stewpots and baking pans, and game could be roasted on a spit. Forward too were other small cabins to accommodate various personnel, clerk, pilot, and engineer. If only a person could feel *safe,* the *New Orleans* wouldn't be a bad boat to be on at all, and she was spacious, too. Sixty to eighty cabin and steerage passengers could be comfortably accommodated.

It was a great day for Wheeling, that day of the steamboat's visit, one Wheelingites were to remember for years and tell their children about. "I remember——," they would say, and local historians, trying to describe how they all felt, would use words like *astonishment* and *delight,* and *admiration,* too, in the old sense of wonder. So it was that the next day, when the fire flowed redly from the furnace and the black smoke issued from the stack, when the soot and chips began falling all over the vessel and on those who crowded around to watch the departure (although most stood well back), when the engine roared and the line was cast off and the boat inched out and the paddle wheels creaked and splashed and the vibration of the engine rocked the deck, Mr. Roosevelt was pleased to be able to retire to the cabin and count out a comfortable return that made the day a good one for the *New Orleans* as well. Maybe, just maybe, a report of this enterprise would stop some of Robert Fulton's continual grumbling about expenses.

No doubt a sense of satisfaction tempered the distaste he usually felt toward making out accounts. He was accustomed to putting off the task as long as possible, however, and it was always tempting to indulge in pleasant fantasies instead, to visualize, for instance, the handsome cabin, with its fine furniture and fittings, filled with well-dressed merchants, with gentlemen traveling for pleasure, with planters whose cargoes filled the hold. It was almost possible to hear bright conversation flowing as freely as the wine, which would be selling at a nice profit, to see passengers nodding in satisfaction over the splendid accommodations, congratulating Mr. Roosevelt on his work and commenting with some awe on the enormous profits the boat must be making. Surely far more interesting to contemplate than rows of dull figures were fantasies in which Nicholas Roosevelt, honored and prosperous, shrugged off the gratitude of a subdued and eclipsed Robert Fulton and the apologies of a suddenly respectful father-in-law.

Now there was another one who was always complaining! Not only in business letters to him but (something a man couldn't help resenting) even to Lydia. The complaints to her were always prefaced with some disclaimer that was supposed to 53 make everything all right—that he knew her husband was virtuous, a man of principle, *but*— That he obviously was devoted to her, *but*— That his optimism was admirable, *but*— But, but, but! It was hard to remember what great friends they once were, for despite all those protestations of continuing regard for him not only as a friend and partner but also as Lydia's husband and his granddaughter's father, there was always that undercurrent of anger.

It had begun almost at once, with little things. They'd been married only two weeks when Latrobe asked Lydia to order some lace for Mary Elizabeth as a surprise, and she had had Nicholas enclose it in a business dispatch instead. You'd think they had committed a crime! Lydia was a blunderer, her father grumbled. She had ruined his surprise, trying to make her husband look good at her own father's expense. And on and on and on. Then there'd been the flatboat voyage, which he would never believe had been anything but a horror for Lydia or that, despite her protestations, it had been she, not Nicholas, who insisted on her going along. It *had* been hard on her, Nicholas had to admit, but good grief! He hadn't tried to get the fever, had he? Lydia was lucky, hardly ever had even a toothache. Unfortunately, Lydia had the dreadful Latrobe habit of writing long, detailed letters to her family about everything that happened, and when she was with them it was talk, talk, talk. So one way or another they'd heard about the two Indians who appeared in the cabin wanting whisky and about her having to bail out the flatboat by herself and about the night spent in the wretched public house in Baton Rouge, with no door between their own miserable cubbyhole and the drunken cutthroats fighting in the next room. She'd given them every detail of the voyage home too, with the yellow fever aboard and the baby almost due, with the captain falling sick and General Wilkinson's nephew dying and everybody looking askance at everyone else for the dreaded signs, the headache and nausea and fever, so that even those who were only seasick were shunned as carriers of the plague. Everything turned out all right, though, as usual. Rosetta was born fine and healthy two weeks after they arrived in New York; the survey was a complete success and convinced Fulton and Livingston to go ahead with the steamboat—and what memories they had! Nicholas smiled, remembering three nights they'd slept huddled together in a buffalo robe on the river bank.

Latrobe didn't like their living with the Marks in New York, either. He didn't like it that his son-in-law seemed not to get along well with his own family (which was no business of his); he couldn't understand what happened to the "very large fortune" to which he believed Roosevelt had been born. Most of all, he didn't like his granddaughter's name. When he and Mary learned that the baby, who had been born in the home of Jacob and Rosetta Mark, was to be named not Mary, not Elizabeth, not Mary Elizabeth, but Rosetta Mark Roosevelt, Latrobe was outraged, considering it a slap at his wife, who, he pointed out to Lydia, had been mother and friend, adviser and protector to her and her brother. They sent dutiful congratulations, inquired anxiously after the infant's welfare and Lydia's, but, "You may name her whatever you please," Latrobe wrote; "I will always call her Mary." And he did. Lydia kept saying he would come around to Rose.

Lydia was probably right. She usually was. In fact, as her husband would have been the first to acknowledge, Lydia was a remarkable young woman. Their marriage, he felt, confirmed his own good judgment. Not only was she wonderfully loyal, she was also a delightful companion, loving the kind of life he loved or willing to share it anyway, with all its troubles and all its risks. That she was talented as well was very nice, although not particularly important for a woman. Uninterested in art himself and clumsy with a pencil ("I do not understand anything of drawing," Roosevelt once wrote to Livingston in apology for a plan he sketched), he was somewhat awed by Lydia's skill in drawing and design and was convinced that if she were a man, she would be as fine an architect as her father. Probably better! She played the organ beautifully, too.

Emerging contentedly from the cabin, Roosevelt saw two of the hands, free of duties, sitting atop the cabin and playing cards. They grinned at him.

"It war a great show, Cap'n!" they called.

Roosevelt, brushed pleasantly by the sharp river breeze, sensing the heightened morale of the crew since the Wheeling triumph—they'd positively swaggered, arguing loftily with those who said the boat would never get past the Falls at Louisville—waved companionably. His men liked and respected him, he knew; it was a nice feeling. They'd seen him sweating with the best of them, recognized his command of every aspect of the boat's workings, from engine to wheel, knew that he himself had taken the soundings that would insure their safe passage, that for him the *New Orleans* had a voice whose every intonation he knew. As he listened with satisfaction to the steady sound of the engines, watched the side paddle wheels that were his special pride dip and rise, dip and rise, felt under his feet the pulsing vibration of power, Nicholas knew that what he had built was good. Here lay his talents, not in the dreary keeping of ledgers and books.

Lydia was staying in the cabin much of the time now, sometimes sewing or playing a game of Patience or reading Parson Weems's *Life of Washington*. The baby was almost due, and they should be reaching Louisville just about in time. There was a good midwife there who had attended Lucy Audubon when she'd had her first child two years earlier at the Indian Queen. But there'd be, Lydia declared, no Indian Queen for her! She had told Nicholas at the time that she thought it was horrible for Lucy. It was a nice enough tavern, and Lucy and John James did have their own room, but they had to go through someone else's sleeping quarters (with four to eight people in it at once) to get to it. There was only the one pump in the courtyard for washing, and the public rooms were full of cigar smoke and spit. She wouldn't have her baby in anybody else's home, either; it had been hard enough at the Marks', good friends though they were. No, the cabin would be a perfectly fine lying-in room, and she'd have her own maids and some decent privacy. Besides, who knew what Rosetta might catch in that unhealthy town?

Nicholas, humoring her, agreed. Childbirth was no affair of his. He did hope she wouldn't have any trouble; she hadn't with Rosetta (he'd not believed it at the time, hearing her, but the midwife had laughed at his concern), and from what he'd been told, the second was usually easier. There was whisky aboard to ease the pain if it got too bad. Some women used laudanum, but it wasn't generally approved of. Most people claimed that trying to ease the agony of childbirth was sinful, that its pain was the price God had set to atone for the sin of Adam. Nicholas hadn't really thought much about it. He had heard it said that the more pain a woman suffered in childbirth, the more she would love her child.

As they approached Marietta the next day—it was Wednesday now, October twenty-third—Lydia joined Nicholas on deck. With the weather favorable—so far they had escaped fog, that peril more deadly than darkness, for it muffled the telltale sound of ripples and distorted shapes—with all hands at their duties and Rosetta happy with her nurse, there was time for them to watch the panorama of the river unfurl, to compare their progress with that made in the flatboat, to reminisce, to plan. Would they stay long in New Orleans? A few months, maybe? Just think, Henry would be there; Papa had sent him down to take charge of the waterworks he was to build. Henry would love showing them the quaint French town that they'd hardly had time to see on their earlier visit. Wouldn't Nicholas be glad to see Henry? Yes, he would. Nicholas liked Henry, as did everyone else, that young man who at nineteen was an accomplished architect and engineer and who would die at twenty-four of yellow fever after helping to engineer the fortifications at the Battle of New Orleans. How long would they stop at Natchez? Zadoc Cramer was there now, hoping to find a cure for his consumption in the warmer climate; he would surely want to hear all about their voyage.

But look! There were people waving now from the town and—how exciting!—the cannon boomed in a fine salute. At the mouth of the Muskingum, the ingenious ferryboat that worked by means of a rope stretching from bank to bank and windlasses on either side was stopped right in the middle, while the passengers watched the *New Orleans* steam by. Lydia and Nicholas 57 did not know it, but just upriver Judge Paul Fearing was clocking them. The *Western Spectator* reported later that from his observation the steamboat "was but fifteen minutes in passing from the foot of the island, just above the town, to past the head of the island, where she disappeared below—a distance of three or three and a half miles—so that she must have gone at the rate of twelve or fourteen miles an hour." "Her appearance," the impressed editor added, "was very elegant and her sailing beyond anything we have ever witnessed."

It was during their stop in Marietta, Lydia remembered, that she had commented on the number of children to be seen along the way and had been told then of Mr. Charles Wells, whose prosperous farm they had passed thirty miles upriver, who had twenty-two children by two wives, as had his tenant, Mr. Scott. Both were outdone, though, by their neighbor, Mr. Gordon, whose children by two wives numbered twenty-eight. Her informant, filled with pride in the fruitfulness of the land and its inhabitants, added that in a ten-mile circuit round about, twenty children had been born to ten women in the year just past, all of them twins. Oh, there'd be passengers enough for the steamboat, he'd said laughingly, if she ever really arrived.

Waving from the deck to the children running along the bank or hugging their mothers' skirts beside a cabin in the woods, Lydia guessed that at least twenty more children had been added to the immediate neighborhood since last they passed, but as she heard Rosetta's giggly laugh from her place aft with the maids and welcomed a lively kick from the impatient child within her, she felt content. She wasn't doing too badly herself. Whether you wanted to say it out loud or not, a woman could have too many children too fast (not that you could do much about it!) as her own mother had had. What had she been like? Lydia had often wondered. Papa said that she herself was much like her, even—the observation had launched Papa on a speculative discourse about heredity—to her scrawly handwriting that now looked just like her mother's, after all the pains Mr. Jaudon had taken to train her in beautiful penmanship.

From right to left on the river, from left to center, avoiding the corpse-makers, those deadly snags that could rip a hull in two, the beckoning sawyers and the sunken wrecks, winding past bars and islands and heading into the chutes, the blue-hulled steamboat followed the channel. In high water the hazards were fewer, the danger less, and the troublesome head winds were helpless against the steamboat's power, but still the meandering Ohio presented challenges, pale promises perhaps, but omens of what lay ahead. At Letart's Rapids, nemesis of the upper Ohio, Lydia stood by the aft mast, holding tight, and watched anxiously as the *New Orleans* mastered the rushing chute, Baker giving the engine a surge of power to carry them over the rapids and through the rough water below. Visible within the chute were the dark spots that told of invisible rocks. The ripples roared like beasts, but only a slight jarring told of the passing of the steamboat over the spot where in the flatboat dishes had fallen to the floor and the furniture been disarranged.

The task of wooding up was undertaken usually in early afternoon, but because the frequent delays lost precious time (each day the hungry furnace devoured all the wood the vessel could carry), Nicholas preferred to purchase fuel whenever possible from settlements along the way. It cost more, naturally, but didn't Fulton and Livingston want him to get to New Orleans as quickly as possible? At Point Pleasant they stopped for an hour, and while the crew toted the wood from Mr. Langtry's store, the hundred inhabitants of the town and the emigrants from back in Virginia who were setting out here for the West hurried to the landing. The town drunkard confined in the pillory next to the whipping post, from which he had a fine view of the river, shouted out a complaint of neglect as the judge and the lawyers, with court dismissed, emerged from the log house of justice next to the log-house jail and passed by him to join the crowd. Those who had it paid their twenty-five cents to come aboard, and some of them even took notes as Mr. Baker explained the machinery, determined, they said, "to make a like machine." They were quite earnest about it, too.

A week after they had left Pittsburgh, Cincinnati lay just ahead, a flourishing town of more than two thousand people 59 where, it was reported, lots on Main Street were selling for as much as two hundred dollars a front foot. Here cabinetmakers and clockmakers, wheelwrights and gunsmiths, bookbinders and shoemakers were busy; Cincinnati pottery was already being shipped by barge to New Orleans and on to Europe as well as the East. Here too emigrants stopped to fill the squalid waterfront boardinghouses before moving on to the valleys of the Miamis. Lydia and Nicholas knew the town well from the flatboat trip, having met through letters of introduction such leading citizens as Dr. Daniel Drake, already at twenty-six gaining fame as the "Franklin of the West"; Jacob Burnet, an eminent lawyer who entertained them at his handsome brick house outside the west end of town; General Harrison, whose farm lay just below Cincinnati, at North Bend. Nicholas suggested tying up here for the night so that he could lay in a supply of beer and porter next morning from the excellent brewery of John Embree at the foot of Race Street, but by now Lydia was nervous, heavy, and cross. She was eager to reach Louisville before the baby came, eager to feel comfortable in the hands of a good midwife. She *wanted* to go on to Louisville, she declared; she did *not* want to waste time here in Cincinnati buying porter for passengers who might or might not materialize a thousand miles farther down. She was tired. Rosetta was tired. In Louisville there would be friends with small children who were waiting to welcome her and her child. They should not waste the remaining hours of daylight dillydallying here when they could be making headway down the river. Maybe they could reach Big Bone Lick Creek, or at least an island near Lawrenceburg where there was a good landing and wood could be got first thing in the morning, and they would reach Louisville the next night.

Usually she acceded to Nicholas's wishes; this time she showed the temper that was usually so well controlled.

They would go on.

Late in the afternoon of Sunday, October 27, 1811, young Philip Bush, who lived with his parents and siblings on a farm in Boone County, Kentucky, opposite North Bend, saw old Mr.

Weldon and his two sons come running from the adjoining farm, waving their arms frantically.

"The British are coming down the river," they cried. "The British are coming!"

It was true, then! The rumors of war were rumors no longer. The British (with their Indian allies? Oh, no!) were already at the door. All of the Bushes rushed to the bank "and behold," Philip wrote later to his old friend Orlando Brown, "the First steamboat that ever navigated the River at that point, making her dignified appearance and slowly marching down the stream, seeming with her lever beams to be warning everything to clear the track—

"My father who was about 44 years old, had never heard of such a thing, but stood looking on, smiling as much at his own ignorance as at the monster of the water.

"We of course let her pass and in wonder & silence returned. The only suggestion that I recollect of being my own That it must be some new kind of a sawmill intended for the West."

On October 30, Cincinnati's *Liberty Hall* noted in Ship News that "the *Steamboat*, lately built at Pittsburgh, passed this town at 5 o'clock in the afternoon, in fine stile [sic], going at the rate of about 10 or 12 miles an hour." And the *Western Spy*, noting her passage, commented, "The Citizens of this place were much disappointed in not having an opportunity of viewing her, only as she passed. She made no stops here. From the rapidity with which she passed this place it is supposed she went at the rate of 12 or 14 miles an hour."

4

At midnight on October 28, in the city of Louisville (at that time all towns were cities, villages towns), most of the fifteen hundred citizens lay sleeping. Some, perhaps, stared into the darkness in despair or were wrapped in passionate embrace or comforted a colicky child. Or lay dying. Or giving birth. Bargemen and keelers from the vessels sheltering at Bear Grass Creek caroused noisily in the waterfront taverns, and around the deserted main buildings, the post office and courthouse, the warehouses and rope walks and the bagging factory, a few furtive figures skulked in the shadows and set the dogs to barking. But over the town lay a forest stillness.

A brilliant moon sharpened all the shadows. It shone on the little town nestled on the bluff seventy feet above the river, its beams fingering in the heavy forest the minuscule dot that was the white man's civilization. It brought out the silver in the river and the silver of the sycamores and birches whose whitened trunks told of winter to come, lighted up the ponds whose miasmic breath had earned for Louisville the label of Graveyard of the West. It lighted up, too, the cascading rapids that foamed and whirled and eddied some five miles below the town, spilling from the great ledge of limestone that extended across the river, a vast reliquary of terebratulites and caryophillites and corallines and other tiny creatures that for millions of years had deposited their carapaces in this place that once was sea. It barely found the thin edge against the wilderness that was Jeffersonville, on the opposite shore, beyond which the limitless forest stretched to no one knew where, save that within it Indians brooded over the encroachments of white men who hypocritically preached brotherhood with red. ("Is there a drop of white blood in this flesh?" cried Tecumseh. "Did a white woman ever breed me a brother, or a white man have an Indian son?" Who was this Great White Father?)

The comet rode high.

The eerie sound shattered the stillness, screeched into the ears of the sleepers, stopped even the tipplers' songs; it could have come from the forest, or from the river's depths, or from the sky. It hurled citizens out of their beds, hurried them into their clothing, screamed panic, screamed fright, screamed British! Indians! Comet! The comet! It was a sound never before heard in this place, by these people. As one called to another, as doors and windows opened and dogs and pigs and cows set up a din, there was no escaping the commotion even if one could sleep through the roar of the escaping steam. And on the river was visible the glow of fire and the lift of sparks and in the light of the moon a vessel—a devil ship?—at the mouth of Bear grass Creek. Or was it the comet fallen? Or visitors therefrom? But some of the people in Louisville knew about steamboats, had heard of the *New Orleans,* remembered Mr. Roosevelt's promise of two years earlier, and, feeling very smug and very wise, reassured their neighbors, promising that they might even go aboard the vessel next day. (Hah! some said.) But no one slept in Louisville the rest of the night.

The arrival had been spectacular, dramatic, wonderfully satisfying! Nicholas loved it. All on board were awake and on deck, even Rosetta, when the steamboat came in. They had not been able to hear the Falls fifteen miles above as they had in the flatboat, for the noise of the engine prevailed, but its roaring had come to them from far around the bend. As they approached the town all hands had gathered, with Baker preparing to lower the fires and the helmsman at the wheel ready to ease the *New Orleans* over to the left to enter the harbor in front of the town, there to join other vessels waiting for a rise in the water at the Falls or, if they were lucky, scheduled to make the passage next day. Here was one of the finest harbors for boats along the Ohio, twelve feet deep even at the driest season and extending a good distance out into the river and down to the middle of Corn Island, past the town, sheltering vessels from wind and ice and from the danger of being carried away by the current should cables give way or the first try at landing fail. Rarely was it uncrowded. Vessels arriving from upriver could be delayed for days or weeks or months awaiting a rise, and hardly would a general exodus empty the harbor than other boats arriving would fill it up again. Keelboats and barges and bateaux coming upriver lodged here after the arduous passage across the Falls by towline,

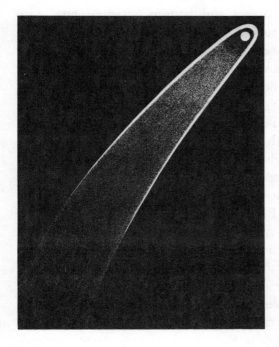

A Royal Observatory illustration of the Great Comet of 1811. From *The Story of the Comets* by George F. Chambers, 1909.

an incredibly laborious process in which a line several hundred to a thousand feet long was fastened to the top of a vessel's mast and the other passed to the crew on shore, with a bridle—a short rope lashed at one end to the bow and at the other end to a ring through which the cordelle, or towline passed—used to keep the boat from swinging. Thus equipped, those hardy boatmen, pulling and heaving, worked the vessel up the rapids and into the safe water of the harbor, where the cargo, which had been unloaded below to be wagoned upward, could be taken on again. Since the rapids were passable only for four months of the year and even in those times varied in depth from ten inches to twelve or fourteen feet, only flatboats could be reasonably sure of passage. Even they often unloaded their cargo above the Falls (not below; the flatboats never came upstream) to lighten the burden and reloaded at the harbor below the Falls.

As the *New Orleans,* shrieking and huffing, rounded to and prepared to throw out lines, torches flared, lights wavered, and agile rivermen leaped over the tops of cabins to look. The lights threw flickering shadows on the clusters of boats, the family boats and keelboats, barges and bateaux, stirring now with frightened occupants suddenly wakened, with crying children, women gathered together, men swearing at this raucous intruder that had come screeching into their rest, swearing again as they heard from the boisterous crewmen of the *New Orleans,* throwing out ropes and preparing to land, shouted insults of greeting to those rivermen they knew. On deck Nicholas and Lydia stood, exulting. Time enough tomorrow to think about low water at the Falls. Time enough then to call for the midwife. (Yes, she was sure, Lydia insisted.) Tomorrow there would be work to be done on the steamboat and people to be met; efforts would be made to persuade Mr. Berthoud and some of the other merchants to ship cargo by way of the *New Orleans,* but tonight there was only triumph and the excitement of making this sensational landing in the night.

They were up at daybreak, eager to see if Louisville had changed since their three-week stay during the flatboat trip. The waterfront looked much the same, with the dram shops and brothels and gambling dens, but visible above in the town proper were several more three-story brick houses, with their parapet walls. One enormous one had been built atop the Indian mound near the big pond, Mr. Gwathmey's, probably. The site of the Croghan home, Locust Grove, was visible, although trees hid the house where they had met the great General George Rogers Clark, Mrs. Croghan's brother. They could see the new, handsome courthouse, just completed, with cupola and spires and its wooden cannon bound with hoops, and what looked like a Roman Catholic chapel on Main Street near Tenth. Yes, the town had grown, but it was pleasantly familiar still. Lydia wondered if it had acquired a bookstore or library since Lucy Audubon lived here; she'd complained about the lack of either one to offer her some diversion while John James tramped around the countryside looking at birds.

They had hardly breakfasted when the first visitors arrived, full of congratulations and honest awe, eager to see those sawmill-looking wheels up close. Some wanted to examine the machinery, and Nicholas, elegant in his blue suit and frilled shirt, freshly shaved, introduced Baker, who showed those interested in gears and beams and valves just how the engine worked while Nicholas and Lydia greeted friends and acquaintances and offered them wine or whisky from the cabin's stores. The crew, relieved temporarily of duty, were already on shore, heading for the dramshops, glorying in attention from giggling girls and predatory women and from other rivermen who were promising they'd have their comeuppance when they tried working the *New Orleans* over the Falls. And how the heck, the other boatmen asked, openly contemptuous, secretly anxious, how the heck did they think they could bring the steamboat *up* against Letart's Falls or Horsetail Ripple, or even against an ordinary current, without setting poles or cordelles? The crewmen, ostensibly confident but secretly anxious themselves, scoffed at the doubters. Just wait! they said. You'll see.

Women visitors, most of them, to Lydia's annoyance, little interested in the mechanics of the boat, tried to draw her aside for whispered questions. How soon? Not on the boat! With the crew about? Oh, my dear, you must come and stay with us.

Childbirth was routine, for most women an annual event.   67

That it was perilous everyone knew, and that death could be the end of it and often was husbands and fathers knew too, but so life was. And about the process were ritual habits, accepted ceremonies. Not many American women (or men) were yet reconciled to the concept of male doctors for delivery, an innovation introduced in Europe a century earlier but even there not widely accepted, save perhaps in London. Male doctors did deliver babies in hospitals or wards for destitute women, where puerperal fever raged and doctors came to the delivery room direct from autopsies, where they wore the same suit, often bloodied, for operations and deliveries, and where the screams of patients undergoing major surgery without anaesthesia and held down by husky medical students echoed through the halls. Here in the West, midwives monopolized the obstetrical field, although in these great distances they were often unavailable and women delivered themselves, sometimes with the help of female relatives or frightened husbands, sometimes not. Wherever or however, on family boats along the rivers, in makeshift shelters in the wilderness, in isolated cabins, or in Louisville homes, they accepted as ordained (or did not—who knew?) their allotted role.

So why should women be interested in engines? Or in how steam worked? Would knowing about it help bear children? Stop the pain? Make easier the hard, anxious days? Rip the deadly membrane of the croup from children's throats? For bearing the children was only the beginning. No, let men tinker. The women did want to see the cabin, and clucked and shook their heads over Lydia's plan to make it a lying-in room. They made much of Rosetta, who hung back shyly at first but soon accepted a proffered hand and walked around with the throng of women as they exclaimed over the convenience of the arrangements, taking a peek at the discreetly curtained "necessary." They told Lydia that she and the children—there would be two of them to consider, remember!—should not even think of going over the rapids even if Mr. Roosevelt insisted on taking the chance himself. Why not wait for the spring freshets? Lydia almost laughed then, thinking of Robert Fulton's rage if they did, but then she became impatient. Her ankles were swollen, her legs ached, her back hurt, the baby was bumping around restlessly as though he, too—she was sure this one would be a boy—were tiring of this conversation. Yes, she answered sharply, as they offered their dire warnings, she and Mr. Roosevelt knew all about the dangers, all about the wrecks. No, they had not been here four years earlier to see the *Tuscarora* and the *Rufus King,* seagoing ships but of smaller burden than the *New Orleans,* founder so spectacularly upon the rocks, although they'd certainly heard about it. And yes, they knew that a third ship, the *Penrose,* had escaped disaster by being cautious and waiting a year. A year!

Well, they were not waiting! Lydia was immediately sorry for her impatience. These were her friends, who really cared, whose concern was genuine. And as they murmured their objections and pressed invitations upon her, she managed to smile, be grateful. Let's see what happens, she said. The water is bound to rise. Let's wait until the baby comes.

Not long now, she told herself, as she retired to the cabin and a welcome respite from the commotion aboard. She could feel it in her back, the beginning twinges of the terrible, splitting pains that would tear her apart, make her scream. No, she would not let them! Nicholas had been so upset the last time; he expected *her* to be the stoic one, the calm one. He couldn't understand that you couldn't help it, that your body was screaming, not you, that you just couldn't believe it, believe the pain, that it wasn't like his toothaches. Everybody said the second one was easier, unless, of course, it hadn't turned properly and the midwife then would have to reach in and turn it around, and if she couldn't, well, that was the end for both of you.

The midwife would be here soon, but Lydia felt with a sudden sharp anguish the absence of her stepmother. She'd wanted her to be there when Rosetta was born, instead of Rosetta Mark, but she would never admit it. To do so would suggest that Nicholas had somehow failed her, and Papa would have something else to hold against him. Oh, if only she weren't always having to make peace!

On the night of October thirtieth, the second day after the arrival of the *New Orleans* at Louisville, Henry Latrobe Roosevelt,

lusty and punctual, came screaming into the world. The birth
was indeed far easier than Rosetta's had been; it was with a relaxed joy and a feeling of pride that Lydia greeted Nicholas when
he came into the cabin. She had given him a son. No matter what
you said, no matter how much they loved their daughters, no
matter how hard it was for a woman to admit it, men were more
delighted, more proud, more excited when a son was born. But
if Nicholas wanted this son to be named after him, he was careful
not to say; he had won on the first choice. Henry Latrobe Roosevelt sounded, he said, like a fine name, and as he took his son
into his arms, Lydia smiled at his satisfied expression, reading
it well. Ebullient with the welcome accorded the vessel along the
way, proud of this newborn son, secretly pleased that low water
at the Falls would delay departure and so give him an opportunity to bask in adulation and to enjoy the festivities planned by
his Louisville friends, Nicholas was supremely content. Moreover, so often had he been reading and hearing reference to the
New Orleans as "Mr. Roosevelt's steamboat," so far away seemed
the complaints and machinations of Fulton and Livingston, that
it was almost possible to believe that to him alone belonged the
credit for the steamboat and with it the honor—if not all the
riches—soon to be earned. And to Lydia, of course, by reflection.
Seeing her now with this second child of their love, sharing her
pride, Nicholas felt a special tenderness—and triumph. Her family's opposition had only made her love him more fiercely; he
wondered if they knew that.

There was to be a public dinner in his honor a few days later, for men only (typical of the West! Lydia thought, recalling
with nostalgia sparkling gatherings in Washington). Other en-
tertainments were planned as well. With the water at the Falls
still too low for passage and no sign of rain upriver, it appeared
that the Roosevelts would be around for a while, and every day
there were visitors to the steamboat. The curious came at least
to gape, old friends came to see the new baby, and anyone passing through town tried to manage an introduction to Mr. Roosevelt and a visit aboard. Much to Lydia's pleasure, Lucy and
John James Audubon and little Victor, two and a half, just come

from Henderson, were stopping in Louisville for a few days before traveling on the thousand miles to Fatland Ford, Lucy's Pennsylvania home. "On horseback!" Lydia exclaimed to Nicholas later. Victor rode in front of his father, who'd decided against their taking the coach because from the coach he would miss the birds along the way. Poor Lucy! Lydia laughed, then had a sudden dreadful thought: Was anyone saying Poor Lydia!?

One visitor Nicholas welcomed was Captain Henry Shreve, the merchant boatbuilder, who was returning from New Orleans on a ninety-five-foot barge with forty hands, intent on being back in Brownsville before *his* wife had *her* baby. He took time to come aboard, and asked so many questions that Nicholas grew testy. He'd expected only acclaim, and some of Shreve's comments sounded almost critical. "Now if the boiler were on deck. . . ," he'd said musingly, and not finished. Or if the cylinders were horizontal. . . . His *Washington,* which would incorporate these changes and set the pattern for western steamboats for a century thereafter, was seven years away.

Nicholas planned to use the dinner given him as an occasion to solicit subscriptions for the Ohio Steamboat Navigation Company now being formed by the three partners for the building of boats to ply the Ohio. It was expected that an outline of the anticipated profit from the *New Orleans,* carefully worked out, would persuade investors that even greater profit could be made on the Ohio and its tributaries, where there was greater population and towns were proliferating. There was hurry, great hurry, for competitors were breathing hard on the necks of the would-be monopolists. Oliver Evans and Daniel French were already challenging their claims, with French running a steamboat at Cooper's Ferry and Evans building a small sternwheeler in an effort to sidestep the Fulton patent; and they were only two. The inventive genius of America had perceived the potential of steam, and like the new lands that were drawing immigrants to the West, the enchanting vistas opened to inventive minds drew them to experiment and explore. No one man now, nor two, could stop what had begun.

The dinner, splendidly attended, was held at the one tavern

that boasted a reception hall of sorts. Lydia saw Nicholas off with a straightening of the lapels of his coat, a flick of an imaginary speck from his snowy white neckcloth, and admonitions to remember everything so that he could give her a full report upon his return.

"And don't let them get too stirred up about politics," she warned, reminding him of Pittsburgh. There, politics was such a sore subject—indeed it was everywhere in America—that social gatherings often ended up in angry exchanges and even challenges to duels. As religion had been the first cause of dissension in the New World, now, as English travelers remarked in astonishment, politics was "the most irritable subject" that could be introduced, even in backwoods communities, where one would think the imperatives of survival precluded other concerns. Because Nicholas had been in Washington in August, everyone would be sure to want to know what the sentiment was in the capital about war with England. Did the people there, Westerners were asking, still think only in terms of a war at sea? Didn't they know that the real trouble was here in the West? Who but the British in Canada were supplying the Indians with arms? Where else were the guns coming from that General Harrison and his men were facing even now at the Prophet's town at the mouth of Tippecanoe Creek on the Wabash?

With the fiery Tecumseh away in the South rallying tribes to his cause, General Harrison had gone on the attack. Fourteen hundred men—regulars, militia, and cavalry—had marched in late September, determined to destroy forever the power of the Prophet and with it the superstitious awe that made fanatics of his followers. It was high time, everyone thought, to end this growing and dangerous movement toward an Indian confederacy, high time to make the Indiana Territory safe for settlement. The men—*western* men—were brave and eager. Only a few days ago a letter had come from a member of the cavalry, written from camp at Burrow, some twenty miles above Vincennes. The cavalry, he wrote with pride, would lead the attack and so "have the honor of smelling the first powder from the Prophet's guns." He and many others could well be smelling it now, charging, dying. And who in the seaboard states gave a darn?

No, if the party got bogged down in politics, Lydia knew there would be little time to talk about the steamboat, although actually even politics was taking second place in the news lately to the comet; there would surely be talk about that. All of the newspapers, the *Louisville Gazette* and the *Journal,* Frankfort's *Palladium,* the *Kentucky Gazette,* and the *American Statesman,* brought in by post from Lexington, were filled with dispatches from New York, from Boston, from London, reporting on the comet's position and direction. Columns were filled with speculation and pronouncements: Was this comet an old one returning? Were comets the residence of rational beings? Was a comet a hot body? A cold one? Was its appearance a sinister portent of disaster? Surely a portent! To quiet widespread apprehension, sober articles discussed the nature of comets and their place in the spectrum of heavenly bodies. Kepler was quoted, and Halley; there were citations from Ferguson's *Astronomy.* But one did not have to be superstitious to be apprehensive. Dr. Halley himself said that had the comet of 1680 been in a slightly different position, had the earth at that time been in the part of her orbit nearest to the node of the comet through which it passed, their mutual gravitation would have caused a change in the plane of the orbit of the earth, and in the length of the year. Had the comet actually struck against the earth, an event he pronounced by no means improbable, "the shock," he said, "might reduce this beautiful frame to its original chaos." And with Sir William Herschel, the eminent British astronomer, estimating the length of this present one's double tail to be more than a hundred million miles in length and its head hundreds of miles across, why, who could fail to be overwhelmed and frightened by such enormity?

Nicholas was impatient with Lydia's conjecturing about what they would talk about. The main topic of conversation would have to be the steamboat, wouldn't it? That's what the dinner was about, after all. And he had a ready supply of conversational material on that subject—the investment opportunity it offered, the time it would save in shipping, its splendid accommodations, everything. And yes, he would tell her all about it when he got home.

73

There were toasts galore at the dinner; Nicholas returned them gracefully. The mayor was there; so was Jared Brooks, editor of the Louisville *Gazette* and an engineer, interested in plans being made for the building of a canal around the Falls. Dr. Richard Ferguson was a guest, and Judge Fortunatus Cosby, of the Jefferson County Circuit Court, and a number of others of equal prominence. Of special concern to Nicholas were the Tarasçon brothers and the Berthouds, merchants and shippers, from whose warehouses merchandise traveled up and down the rivers and whose commitment to steam could make a difference in the prospects of the Ohio Company.

Liquor flowed freely—Louisville was acquiring a reputation as a liquor emporium—and Nicholas, flushed with attention and with wine, came almost to quarreling with those skeptics among his hosts who, even while they applauded his having come down the river, would not believe that the steamboat would ever go up. In fact, they doubted that she would even go *down* now, with the Falls to pass. Anyway, inquired one of the more truculent, how could there ever be enough vessels to carry on the enormous trade Mr. Roosevelt envisioned if only Fulton and Livingston were allowed to build and run them?

"We are building more boats, gentlemen!" Nicholas exlaimed. It was the perfect opening for his appeal for subscriptions. "*You* can be part of our corporation." But no one seemed eager to invest. They would wait and see. As if by prior accord, the conversation was turned to other topics. How was Mrs. Roosevelt? What did he think of the progress Louisville had made since his last visit? Of the new buildings? Of the appointment of two policemen to curb lawlessness? Had he heard there would be a branch of the State Bank in Louisville within the next year? Main Street would soon be paved. . . .

Barely a week later, the water still being low, Mr. Roosevelt entertained at dinner aboard the *New Orleans,* and he had plans for making the occasion a memorable one. The guests, most of whom had been his hosts at the earlier party, came elegantly dressed. The uninvited—the rivermen aboard the barges in the harbor and some upward bound who had come over from Shippingport, immigrant families delayed at the rapids and eager for diversion, townspeople fascinated by the steamboat or simply attracted to spectacle—watched as the visitors were ushered aboard. The vessel was a familiar sight now, but still interesting, and the hands were known by now, too. Hardly did they appear on shore before the challenges began, the questioning: "How you gonna keep her from blowin' up?" "Man, that ol' Mississippi ain't gonna give you a chance!" The crew, more confident than when they left Pittsburgh, tossed off the questions, but once in a while, before the evening's whisky had drowned any doubts, their tone was less sure. They too knew about the wicked river.

After greeting the guests with Nicholas, Lydia retired to the ladies' cabin with the children and the maids. For a short time, the men stood on deck, envisioning a Louisville of the future as Roosevelt was describing it, waving his arm toward the town in a great sweep. It would be a great junction, a metropolis, with factories, shops, with a harbor filled with steamboats taking on cargo from warehouses on shore, unloading upriver merchandise, taking on goods for their return trip, their ranks of smoke stacks sending banners of prosperity into the sky. Not only a promoter but a true believer, too, Nicholas was eloquent. Imagine! he told them. Steamboats racing up and down the Ohio, along the Kentucky, the Wabash, the Tennessee; easy, comfortable passage to and from Pittsburgh, Wheeling, the East; passengers stopping at Louisville, settling; immigrants pouring in to establish new farms, to grow produce that called for more shipping. More inns would be needed, more lumber, more tools; the city would expand, and the state too, its political power growing with its population. There would be new brick houses on the hills. . . . Imagine. . . .

They did, each seeing his own vision—the banker, the merchant, the politician, each dreaming his own dream. Then, as they turned and looked upstream and saw the flow of that relentless current against which all the power man could summon could do so little and that so slowly, they shook their heads. Steam engines could work a pump, even the machinery of a mill, but against a counterforce? Some laughed. And as they moved 75 toward the forward cabin and looked downstream, they saw there to convince them the vivid, ever-present reminder of the power of that stream, the tumbling, dangerous rapids.

The cook had outdone himself. There were fish from the river, fresh game roasted on the spit, fine wines freely flowing. As the dinner progressed and toasts were drunk, conversation, too, flowed easily, turning to many topics and a few ribald jokes. Talk of politics brought on louder and louder discussion, but Nicholas skillfully turned it from outright argument and the guests relaxed, feeling expanded and expansive as more Madeira was poured and excellent cigars were passed. Fragrant smoke was wafted upward; Mr. Roosevelt was complimented on his choice of wines and on the elegance of the cabin's appointments. A fine vessel! No question about it, if only one could feel—There was a lull in the conversation, and all of the company became conscious at once of a steady rumbling noise. Thunder? They looked at one another in some surprise. There had been no sign of rain, no darkening of the sky; perhaps there would be a rise in the water sooner than expected. They all felt it at once then, a vibration, movement, heard the steady, rhythmic thumping, a splashing—up, down, up, down—Help! The boat was in motion! She had slipped her anchor; she was drifting toward the Falls!

Glasses crashed; elegant suits were bespattered with wine; cigars dropped from trembling hands and burned holes in the cloth, slid dangerously to the table's edge. Quick thinkers grabbed them, rushed with the others out on deck even as they realized that Roosevelt was calling out that there was no cause for alarm. (Idiot!) Some yanked at their neatly pressed coats, prepared to leap overboard, and looked with fear toward the Falls over which the *New Orleans* would never be able to pass with the water so low. The Falls were receding! They were farther away than before, were behind them, farther and farther away. The steamboat was headed upstream, against the current, moving faster and faster, the engine warming to its work, steam blowing off at the safety valve, the vessel seeming to take on a life of her own, with the paddle wheels churning and the vibrations growing stronger and the water sloshing and falling with each turn of the wheels. Ahead lay Six Mile Island. Ahead lay Wheeling, Cincinnati, Pittsburgh. Ahead? Ahead lay the future.

When Nicholas, laughing, delighted, told Lydia later of the consternation and the hurried exit, of the relief and surprise and the chagrin as they admitted they'd been wrong, she clapped her hands, then acknowledged that she had peeked; she couldn't resist, for she had known of the plan beforehand. She had kept Rosetta quiet and Henry was asleep and she'd seen them all go rushing out of the cabin. When he tried to stop them, they'd thought he was demented! Oh, the surprise excursion had been a wonderful idea! She hugged him, told Rosetta how brilliant her father was.

Now, he said, I'll show those doubters in Cincinnati.

First, though, there were other trips out of Louisville. Those who had not been at the dinner had to be given the chance for a ride on the steamboat. For the nominal price of one dollar per person, several excursions were taken to Six Mile Island and back. The returns were duly entered in Mr. Roosevelt's accounts, and Jared Brooks recognized that the successful demonstrations merited more than a mere mention in his weekly news articles. Early in November, therefore, a paragraph appeared that was widely copied all over the nation a week or so later, depending on the speed of the post.

> Arrived at this place on the 28 ult. Mr. Roosevelt's steamboat *New Orleans*. We are informed she is intended as a packet boat between Natchez and New Orleans; her burthen is 405 tons, and can accommodate from 60 to 80 cabin and steerage passengers, in a style not inferior to any packet in the union. She arrived at this place in 65 hours sailing from Pittsburgh. Frequent experiments of her performance have been made against the current, since her arrival; in the presence of a number of respectable gentlemen, who have ascertained with certainty she runs thirteen miles in two hours and a half.

The visit to Cincinnati was planned for late in November. Daily soundings at the Falls showed no increase in the depth of the water, and although there was beginning to be a strange sultriness to the air that might augur a change in the weather, there   77 was no sign of rain. Friends in Cincinnati had sent word that they felt discriminated against, and there were hints that some might consider buying shares in the Ohio Steamboat Navigation Company, so that a visit there would be both useful and pleasurable. Lydia was feeling stronger now and looked forward to seeing their friends and showing off the children. Nicholas planned conferences with such business people as Messrs. Baum and Perry, whose line of barges cried for steam power, and with Mr. Hurdus, who had a cotton manufactory. Surely, too, a trip upriver to Cincinnati would silence the skeptics forever!

Their reception in the upriver town was warm and satisfying. All doubts were dispelled now, and hundreds of citizens were delighted to take passage on the steamboat, at one dollar per person, for short excursions to Columbia, at the mouth of the Little Miami. On nearly every trip the boat was filled to capacity with admiring visitors who exclaimed over the workings of the engine, watched fascinated the movement of the paddle wheels, and asked endless questions of Baker and Jack, for whom so short and familiar a journey was sufficiently routine to allow them to relax and enjoy the attention. A week seemed all too short a stay, but the water showed signs of rising, and on December fourth *Liberty Hall* took note of the steamboat's imminent departure.

> *The Steam Boat*
>
> Arrived here on Wednesday last, in 45 hours from the falls, a distance of 180 miles, against the current of the Ohio. To the citizens of this place, it is an object of much curiosity.
>
> Several short trips have been performed up and down the river from this place, and numbers have gratified themselves by taking passage in these short voyages. On the rise of water, she will sail for her place of destination, it is said, to return to us no more.

Back in Louisville, they waited still. A greater sensation had diminished interest in the *New Orleans;* all the talk now was of the battle of Tippecanoe. From the battlefield came dispatches giving lists of the casualties: Colonel Davies, dead; Colonel Abraham Owen, dead; Judge Taylor of Jeffersonville, wounded; Governor Harrison lucky enough to receive a shot through his hat, which scratched the side of his head; many of the cavalry and militia, dead. *Now,* thundered the *Courier,* "Will our government act, or will they always sleep?" The steamboat was yesterday's news.

Nicholas was becoming edgy; late December could bring ice, and even the camaraderie of the people of Louisville was beginning to pall. The daily soundings continued, but the water would not rise; there was no sign of rain, and the air was still. Nothing seemed to move save the river itself, going grumbling and churning over the ledge. The crew grew restless, the children fretful, even Lydia cross. She took the children with her into town to visit and returned angry. People were saying the *New Orleans* would be here until spring, that the Roosevelts might have bitten off more than they could chew. The Falls had kept vessels lighter than theirs waiting on its whims, waiting as long as a year. They ought to settle down for the winter, be glad they'd come this far.

Nicholas had been hearing the same things. It was the blasted river, he said; it seemed to be deliberately frustrating them. Or the weather, the oppressiveness. Nobody could help becoming dispirited; the air was like lead.

The rise was hardly perceptible at first, just a little less of the rocks showing, a barely visible change in the depth of the channels. The flatboats left first, needing little more than inches for passage; some of the keelboats followed, sending their freight around by wagon to Shippingport. The licensed pilots were busy, the town's coffers filling with the two dollar fees for their services. Most of the vessels were using the middle chute; the preferred one, the Indian, was not yet passable. Each day the water rose a little more, a little more; each day Nicholas himself took soundings, studied the looks of the channels, watched as other boats took the chutes. Barges were beginning to pass now, some of them requiring almost four feet for passage. The *New Orleans* drew four. And finally he decided that the time had come. The depth of the water exceeded by five inches—five inches—the draught of the boat. It was a narrow margin, dangerously narrow;   79 by all precedent, all good judgment, they should wait for higher water, wait another day, two days. But there was still no sign of rain, only that same leaden sky. Any morning could bring not a rise but a fatal drop that could last until the river was closed by ice.

Tomorrow, Nicholas said. Tomorrow.

5

It would take them forty-five minutes to go over the Falls of the Ohio; they would cross four hundred million years of time. This ledge, this fossil bed of billions, trillions of small shelled creatures that lived deep in a Devonian sea, had risen in some great regional uplift of ancient times to become a reef, a reef originally as solid and immense as the Great Barrier Reef on the other side of a later world. Over it, for millennia, seas ebbed and flowed; into them flowed rivers that drained the continent above.

Eons passed.

Then, long ago, but only this morning in geologic time, glacial shields began moving slowly, slowly down from the north, spreading their mighty weight across the land and rivers, a weight from which the earth is rising still. After they receded—again so slowly!—their outwash filled the bed of one of these ancient rivers so that when its stream flowed free once more it had to cut a new channel to the north of the old, leaving a fertile plain where its earlier bed had been. Thousands of years after the first humans walked upon that plain, a town would be built upon it.

Meantime, with its old sea gone, the river had to find a new beneficiary for its bountiful gift of waters. Flowing westward, it found a brash new river—or an older, smaller one taking advantage of an opening—rushing down a new-formed valley to the south. Into this river the old one emptied its waters, content, after its long autonomy, to become a tributary stream. In the way of its comfortable westward flow, though, was the ledge, remnant of that ancient reef.

For ages the river fretted at the barrier, pushing its way over and around it, seeking to wear it down as it had worn down other obstacles, a fragment here, a pebble there, a fraction of an inch over a century. Sand and gravel came along to help it erode the calcareous mass; it had aid from airborne particles that weathered the surface rocks; ice helped too—ice was splendid. By the time humans came upon the land, the ledge had been worn down to a remnant of its former self. When the river was high, swollen by rains, it careened triumphantly over the ledge, carrying with it whatever chose, or sometimes what did not choose, to join it. When the river was low, it wound its way through the three channels it had dug in its constant war of attrition. Some day the ledge would be defeated. But not now. Not yet.

The old river didn't care what it carried to the new river beyond. Rafts and floating debris, bodies, sailing ships—the river to which it paid tribute could have them all, do what it would with them. All such things the Ohio was accustomed to; none disturbed its serenity—or had not before. Now, though, a new kind of burden, a most disturbing burden, was bothering it, pushing her way along as though the river had no say about her course. She had managed to push her broad beam through narrow channels that had defeated smaller boats, had passed over formidable sandbars with a surge of her impudent power, rounded the tips of islands that were supposed to be cleverly hidden, overridden wrecks, frightened the fish in the water and the birds along the shore with her racketing wheels, marred the river's clean water and the air above with unnatural, evil droppings, churned up water meant to flow smoothly. And now she was daring the rapids, with five inches of water to spare.

* * *

They would take the Indian Chute, northward, to the right of Goose Island. Deepest of the three, smooth and fast, it was bordered by jagged limestone that lay perilously close to the channel; just under those five inches of grace lurked two deadly rocks just fifteen feet apart. The middle chute, safe and easy for smaller boats, was too narrow for the *New Orleans;* the Kentucky Chute, between Rock Island and the Kentucky shore, narrower still. There was no choice—save not to go.

That choice, not to go, had been urged upon them so freely that Lydia felt she was back in Pittsburgh. Even more freely, and even by Nicholas, she was urged to go by carriage with the children to Shippingport and wait there until the dangerous crossing was accomplished. She agreed to have the children taken there. They would go with friends, as would the two maids, who, Lydia knew, were terrified of the prospect of the passage over the rapids, but she—? She would stay with Nicholas. Her determination, she admitted to herself and to him, too, when he became insistent about her not taking the terrible risk, came not just from loyalty or even from love: She just couldn't bear to miss the adventure! He hugged her hard then, and laughed. *That* was what you couldn't explain to people about him, about her, about *them.*

Whatever their concern, the people of Louisville were not going to miss the spectacle. They would watch from windows that had a view of the river, and few did not. They would take up vantage points along the shores on either side of the Falls or gather on the terraces that rose toward Louisville and toward Jeffersonville on the opposite bank, watch too from Shippingport and Clarksville below. The continuing contest between man and the river was a vital part of their lives, an ever-unfolding drama they watched from the perspective of discriminating judges who knew the river's power and its moods, who had seen vessels founder at their doorstep and could recognize a pilot's skill. This particular contest had a special appeal because of its novelty, and as soon as word got around that the *New Orleans* would leave the next day, December 8, the air was charged with a sense of excited anticipation much like that created by the prospect of bear bait- 83 ings or public hangings. Whatever its basic drama, western life could be drearily routine.

All of them hoped the steamboat would win—or claimed they did, really thought they did, but there were those who felt deep down a delicious frisson at the thought of a vanquished vessel helpless on the rocks, her brazen huffing and puffing silenced, her owners' pretensions punctured. For there were shippers who bitterly resented the threat presented by the Fulton-Livingston monopoly, as well as builders and suppliers who feared that a successful demonstration of the power of steam on the rivers would cut sharply into their profitable barge and flatboat trade. There were also a few who had been guests at Mr. Roosevelt's dinner and still felt a lingering sense of chagrin at their humiliation. To them his confidence seemed only arrogance. And, inevitably, there were the diehard skeptics who would feel, no matter what their honest concern for the Roosevelts, a certain satisfaction if the steamboat should fail. But who would admit to that?

Velocity was the key to safe passage. The momentum of the vessel had to be greater than that of the current, or the helmsman would be at its mercy. For the two-mile run through the winding, narrow channel, dropping down twenty-two feet, the *New Orleans* must exceed the fourteen miles an hour at which the river flowed over the ledge. Andrew Jack, for all his skill, would not be allowed to make the crucial decisions. Several years earlier, so frequent had been the casualties at the Falls, so many wrecks obstructed passage, that the cities of Louisville in Kentucky and Jeffersonville in Indiana Territory had decreed that only court-appointed pilots, to be always available, should conduct vessels over the rapids. For each vessel the pilots were paid a fee of two dollars and—a salutary precaution—were responsible for any damage due to neglect or mismanagement.

It was on this issue of responsibility that the head pilot took issue with Mr. Roosevelt. In his judgment, five inches was too small a margin for safety; the *New Orleans* was an untried vessel, and frankly, he did not think steam power could be relied on under such hazardous conditions. None of the licensed pilots was willing to be responsible for her safe passage, and he rather doubted that any would be willing to take the chance on his own life, either. No, Mr. Roosevelt would just have to wait; others, with more valuable cargoes (what was the hurry, after all?), had waited for as long as a year. There was no arguing with the river, with the sky, with the Lord, was there?

Mr. Roosevelt thought there was. He knew that tomorrow the water could start falling instead of continuing to rise, for there was no sign of rain. The brooding, lowering sky, cloudless but heavy, seemed implacable, permanently fixed in its sullen mood. The December air was thick and unseasonably warm, the sun dull, like a globe of red-hot iron in a mist. The brooding stillness in the atmosphere made one feel like screaming, Do something! Do something! and people were irritable and quarrelsome. The crew began picking fights in the taverns. One way lay open.

An owner who would take full responsibility for damages and who could find a licensed pilot willing to come aboard could depart at his pleasure. And Nicholas Roosevelt was Dutch—Dutch-stubborn, some said. Lydia, seeing his lips tighten, put her hand on his arm. She should stop him, she knew. If there were damages to the *New Orleans,* Robert Fulton would be furious and would surely refuse to pay. It would mean another debt for Nicholas, with the others yet unpaid; it could mean his ruin, the wreck, literally the wreck, of all their hopes. For a moment they looked at each other in silence; then she took her hand away.

"We're going, aren't we?" she said.

On ordinary vessels going over the Falls, additional hands were usually employed to man the oars to ensure the velocity needed for passage. That the *New Orleans* did not require them made the rivermen who were in town even more hostile, but no more than anyone else would they miss the show. A number of them stood on the bank along with those Louisvillians who were not watching from up above or farther along the road that bordered the river as the *New Orleans,* belching great columns of black smoke, weighed anchor in Bear Grass harbor. Slowly she began the wide circuit that would take her half a mile above her anchorage and then, heading downstream, into the swift, impatient current of the Indiana channel. Lydia, with Tiger circling nervously beside her, stood in the stern. Nicholas paced near the bow, where Andrew Jack had taken his place beside the court-appointed pilot. They would guide the helmsmen by hand motion, for there would be no voice communication once the passage was begun. Even before entry into the swirling waters, the wild roar of the Falls would drown out any sound.

In the engine room, Nicholas Baker was watching intently every turn of the engine, checking the water level, listening to every throb of the piston, giving orders to the crew. Andrew Jack may have had to give up his authority, but Baker had not. On the behavior of the machinery, he knew, depended successful passage as surely as upon the skill of the pilots. During the preceding days he had seen to it that the boiler was thoroughly cleaned (even on the relatively clear Ohio, muddy water drawn in by the supply pump could cause problems in the condenser), had checked the boiler head for cracks, tested joints and rivets and given careful instructions to the hands, seen to the fuel supply for the ravenous furnace. And from Mrs. Roosevelt's pretty maid, before she left with the children, there may well have been a final smile and a whispered, "Now you be careful, Mr. Baker!" to fire his heart as well. For in these weeks of shared adventure the attraction between them had been growing into love. He peered at the gauge cocks, checked the supply pump. He was ready.

Nicholas Roosevelt, his apprehension known only to his wife, stood on deck, head high and wide shoulders braced. Here was the test. If the steamboat passed the Falls in glory, there should be no other trial along the way that she could not meet with confidence. He saw the two pilots in the bow look toward each other for an instant and nod. They were ready. He was.

In the stern, Lydia put her hand on Tiger's big head and took a last look at the rapids as the helmsman swung the vessel around to bring her into the basin, heading toward the chute. She whispered a prayer. She was ready.

Even as the *New Orleans* straightened in the stream, those aboard could feel the swift, startling surge of the river's power, could sense the ease with which it would push them, pull them, throw them, bury them if they did not accelerate beyond its grasp. Around the boat the noise of the rushing waters was louder than the hiss of steam and the beat of piston and the splash and creak of paddle wheels. No sooner did they begin their descent than mist, like smoke, swirled around them, rose to mingle with the heavy black smoke from the stack billowing toward the leaden sky. Waves dashed against the vessel, the water eddied and danced and whirled and foamed and enveloped them all in a cloud of pelting water that soaked them to the skin. Seen from the shore, the tumbling waters had appeared more manageable, less fierce; here within them, they were overwhelming, a terrifying force. And then they entered the chute.

Brave and poised, the steamboat lay for a tremulous instant at its head, quivered and shook as in the engine room Baker put upon the boiler all the steam it could bear. The wheels revolved faster and faster, faster than ever before, propelled by the swift current and the goading of the engine; the safety valve shrieked, the boiler roared. And then the vessel slipped into the sleek black ribbon of the channel, lined with those ancient rocks.

Aboard, each one on deck instinctively grasped the nearest object; Lydia, with a quick gasp, held on to the stern rail as Tiger crouched at her feet. The pilots at the bow were motioning to the man at the helm—here, now there, over a little, to the right, to the left, straight ahead! Straight ahead! The vessel seemed out of control, seemed doomed to perish on the black ledges of rock that appeared and disappeared, reached for her, fell back. There was a slight scrape; looking down and back, Lydia could see a rough limestone boulder just beneath the surface of the raging water. The din was frightening; the spray hurled itself at the anxious figures, threw water over the deck, leaped toward the rising smoke. She could sense Tiger's fear as he crouched at her feet, knew her own was hardly less. Thoughts and impressions careened through her mind. Would the lovely blue hull emerge unscathed? Nicholas's daring bring success?—or disaster? Were the children safe? Were they waiting on shore? Oh, how much could go through one's mind in so short a time!

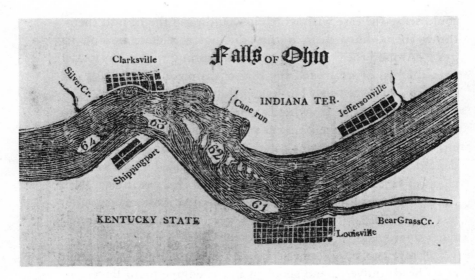

The Falls of the Ohio as shown in *The Navigator* by Zadoc Cramer, edition of 1817. The numbers indicate islands, most of which had popular names. Number 61 was known as Corn Island. Courtesy of The Rare Book Collection, Tulane University.

They were taking the chute, following its narrow, winding bed, skirting the rocks, were flying! She held her breath for what she knew from the flatboat voyage must come next, that instant of taking the big fall and the feeling of lurching descent that would come at the most precipitous drop. Swiftly she leaned down and grasped Tiger's thick coat, feeling reassurance in having another living creature to share her fear.

It came. That sudden, sick feeling as the boat pitched forward, that breath-stopping moment, the exquisite, awful sensation of being suspended over a reaching void, and then—the shock of calm, serenity.

They had passed. With five inches to spare, with just five inches of water more than the draught of the boat, with the great weight of her engine and the depth of her hold, with no sails and no oars and no precedent, the *New Orleans* had ridden the Falls.

She floated triumphant, quiet, the boiler no longer roaring, the smoke from the stack blowing out fitfully, wisps floating hither and yon in the windless, mournful sky. That sky—why wouldn't *it* show a little excitement? The whole universe should celebrate! Lydia, ecstatic, hugged Tiger, who rose and shook himself, spraying water all over her, water that didn't matter now; she couldn't be wetter than she was. She looked up and saw Nicholas and held out her arms.

"Thank God!" They said it together. He closed her hands together in his own, held them, and then there was no time for private celebrations. Proudly he looked toward the shores where spectators were gathered now to see the *New Orleans* round to at the foot of the Falls. As the vessel moved slowly toward the landing at Shippingport, with its bold shore and deep water, other boats pulled close. There were shouts of congratulation; arms were waving, people running. Standing beside Nicholas, the court-appointed Falls pilot who had dared what others would not grinned broadly. They'd all be after him now, by golly! That Mr. Roosevelt was a smart man. As Nicholas complimented him on his skill and with businesslike briskness paid him his fee, plus a bonus, the pilot shook his head, still amazed. Who'd ever have believed it?

The *New Orleans* made her landing a little below the several barges and keelboats already anchored. Lydia, moving over to the railing and scanning the welcoming crowds, saw what she was looking for, a carriage coming along the mud path that led down to the shore and within it a woman waving wildly and a little girl jumping up and down. Henry, she guessed, was asleep in his nurse's arms. Her heart turned over with a surge of tenderness and relief. Now they would all be together as she had prayed, and soon, after supplies were taken on and Nicholas pronounced the boat ready for the fourteen-hundred-mile voyage ahead, they would be on their way!

Waiting at the landing was Mr. James Berthoud, whose house was the handsomest in Shippingport and who always seemed to feel avuncular concern for Lydia. He had been quite cross with Nicholas for allowing her to make the dangerous passage. As the carriage with the children in it came near, he beamed and pointed to one of his boats, which was standing by   *89* with a crew to take them out to the *New Orleans*. Everyone had been so thoughtful. It would not be easy to leave this place where so much had happened and so many new friends had been made and their son had been born; it could be years before they visited Louisville again, transportation being what it was. Some day, perhaps, thanks in some part to this voyage, travel from place to place in America would not be so difficult, would take weeks instead of months, and people could be closer, more *one*.

They were to stay at Shippingport for several days to take on supplies—bread and bacon and other such staples as could not be obtained along the way, as well as all the wood they could carry. Fresh produce could be bought at settlements along the Ohio and game could be shot for the wanting, but along the Mississippi it would not be so easy. With no settlement of any consequence between New Madrid in Missouri Territory and Natchez far below, they would have to depend on their own resources. The wood might last until they reached Yellow Bank, about a hundred and fifty miles downriver, where the two mines were to which Nicholas had purchased the rights from Indiana Territory and from Kentucky; but to carry enough wood, or even coal, to last much longer than a day was almost impossible unless one was willing to increase the draught of the vessel and with it the danger of being stranded on sandbars and shoals. The amount of fuel the furnace consumed, six cords of wood in twenty-four hours, was enormous for the power it produced, much of that power dissipated into the sky in those great clouds of smoke and steam that created awe along the river.

As important as taking on supplies was the careful inspection of the steamboat for any damage done during her strenuous passage over the rapids. Boiler, condenser, supply pump, paddle wheels—all the parts on whose functioning the success of the voyage depended—had to be checked for loosened joints or any other weaknesses the river could exploit. The crew were kept busy cleaning and oiling while Nicholas, along with Andrew Jack, conferred with pilots and other rivermen who had recently come upriver, revising the charting of the lower waters. Where had the channel changed along the Ohio? The Mississippi? What chutes were now blocked by snags? The steamboat could be trapped for months in a chute, in the utter solitude of a watery passage hung with vines and shadows. There could be no backing out once the entry was made. Where had shoals developed? What long-time marks—dead trees, cast-up wrecks, projecting points— were no longer there? Where had new eddies formed? Boils? How fast was the current at Grand Cut Off? Carefully the new data were entered; carefully they studied them, Jack and Nicholas.

Lydia seized the opportunity to do a little visiting, taking Rosetta and Henry with her to show off and to give them some playtime with other children, but the visiting quickly palled. She was eager to be gone now, as was Nicholas, and the crew was becoming restive. Drinking at night with their fellows in the taverns ashore, they heard tales of strange happenings down-river, tales that had been bruited about in Pittsburgh but largely discounted. Evidently there was a feeling of apprehension in the valley about possible Indian attacks, particularly along the Mississippi, where news of Governor Harrison's victory over the Prophet at Tippecanoe on November 7 had not yet come when the rivermen passed. Most of them heard of it only now, a month later, on their arrival at Louisville. This particular fear, though, seemed to be only one element of a general malaise, aggravated by the strange nature of the weather. Around the mouth of the Ohio, where frequent thunderstorms were the rule, there had not been one in over a year; only when such storms were absent did one realize how desperately they were needed to clear the air. The comet had the people downriver, especially in the backwoods, terrified; with the floods and the sickness and everything else, they were imagining portents of disaster everywhere. Woodsmen told of deer suddenly bold or standing immobile before the hunter and of the sudden, unprovoked flights of birds, flights frenzied rather than patterned as they usually were. Squirrels were migrating in unusual numbers; their corpses littered the rivers so that the water was almost unpalatable. Rivermen told of great crowds of people assembling at camp meetings in the woods, coming from as far as a hundred miles away, all of them scared to death. They told of these meetings—a favorite target for wild, brawling *91* attacks by liquored-up boatmen—with their customary derision, and yet they shook their heads, perplexed. A group of them, they said, had invaded a meeting upriver from Natchez, but nobody'd even skedaddled when they came, just stood there and let themselves be bloodied up. It sort of took the fun out of it. The preacher, a big fellow, kept thundering on about how they'd all go to Hades until somebody took a plank to him. The whole thing gave you the willies.

The crew laughed at the stories, but they kept on talking about them, scoffing a little too vehemently. Nicholas knew that it was time to go.

They left at six o'clock on the morning of Friday, December thirteenth. Even so early, the air was heavy, the weather unseasonably warm, but the excitement of leaving and the flurry of preparation lifted spirits and brightened voices, stirred laughter. How could anyone feel anything but hopeful, buoyantly hopeful, after successfully passing the Falls?

Every day, all manner of vessels set out from Shippingport, but even the most jaded Kentuckians were interested in seeing the departure of the *New Orleans*. Friends were there, some who had walked or ridden over from Louisville: Major Croghan and Doctor William Galt, and red-headed William Clark, famous for his great expedition to the West with Meriwether Lewis, who was staying at Mulberry Hill. As one who had seen more than most other men of the land's far reaches, he realized as few others did the importance of the steamboat to the nation's future. He had seen the West, seen its rivers; and he did not agree with the view so many held that the Louisiana Territory, largely barren, would never be widely settled, even if (as was unlikely) the population of the United States expanded to the point where it would need more land than it already had. Mr. Berthoud and other residents of Shippingport were there; across the river, throngs were gathered at Clarksville's landing. One of the Tarascón brothers' twelve-oared barges, with its French crew, which had brought goods down from Pittsburgh and was heading for New Orleans, had been scheduled to leave at first light, but Louis Tarascón was sympathetic to the rivermen's interest in the steamboat and held it back. After all, on the month-long voyage down to New Orleans, a couple of hours would make little difference. Its crew lounged atop the roof of the cabin, spitting tobacco juice and jeering the steamboat's men as they reeled in the cable. We'll get to New Orleans first! they called. Just wait and see.

Other boats were loading too; the waterfront was always busy. Kegs and barrels were piled high on the wharves, holding whiskey and flour and iron castings, millstones and glass. Wooden cages rising in tiers held chickens and turkeys, and tobacco casks, rolled to the wharves by horses by means of shafts fastened to axles through the casks, stood one on top of another. Boats up from New Orleans were unloading exotic wares brought from the West Indies and Europe, molasses and chinaware and fabrics and tea; others were taking on more mundane goods for down-river ports. But as the *New Orleans* gathered steam and departure became imminent, nearly all ashore stopped whatever they were doing to watch. Slaves, worth five hundred dollars each in Louisville and contracted out for wharf work, paused to gape at the fierce surging of coal-black smoke, as did the red-shirted keelers and bargers, unceremoniously setting down crates and boxes. Even the elegantly dressed merchants in frock coats and beaver hats who were overseeing the loading of their vessels motioned to their hirelings to wait until the steamboat had gone.

Smoke poured out, the steam pushed at the safety valve; Jack manned the wheel. Lydia, standing on the stern deck holding Henry while Rosetta stood at the railing and peeked over as much as she could with her nurse's watchful eyes upon her, felt a flutter of pride every time she caught sight of Nicholas passing from engine room to deck and back again or standing near her giving orders to the crew. He was so exactly *right*. Careless he might be with his accounts, heedless of the need for prudence, but in the exercise of his true vocation he was superb. When she had time to ponder, Lydia could almost see why her father criticized him. The Latrobes operated differently, had different values. Nicholas had no interest in the philosophical implications of his undertakings. Would steam change society? Was it good 93 or bad? He did not care. At dinners at the Latrobe family home, when the talk turned speculative, Nicholas was bored. Did it work? he asked. How could it work better? Could it make a profit? He was as pragmatic as the country itself, as uninterested in abstract moral issues as the engines he made, and Lydia, whose Latrobe-ness was an essential part of her being, marveled at the attraction he had always had for her. She knew only that without him not only life but she herself was dull.

Shifting Henry to the other shoulder, she waved gaily at those watching from shore, shaking her head to indicate that she was not the least bit worried. Why, they were more concerned than she about the dangers ahead. The flatboat had traveled the river they called wicked and come through unscathed; surely the steamboat, bigger and faster and stronger, would be able to cope.

The lines were cast off, the anchor weighed, and the *New Orleans* made the great turn that headed her into the channel, then caught the current. It would carry her due west now, hurrying her, hurrying all of them toward their rendezvous with the greater river, the wicked river, and whatever it had in store.

The shore cannon boomed.

6

Indian eyes watched from the forest. Indian voices mingled. *Penelore,* they called her, the Fire Canoe. The shaman chanted.

The river was running faster now, free of the ledge that damned its eagerness above. Past hills and lowlands, past settlements and forest, it carried its gift of waters to the river beyond, taking with it the largesse of creeks and rivers that sacrificially emptied themselves into the broader stream. Past the Salt and the Big Blue, past creeks named Otter and Helen's and Buck, past Doe Run and Little Yellow Bank Creek the river flowed. At Flint Island, ninety miles past the Falls, it paused a little for breath, its channel dividing, its waters just brushing the sandbar that lay to the left below, a sandbar excelling at reminding ambitious vessels not to presume on the Ohio's good will. Even the proud *Tuscarora,* unchastened by her disaster at the Falls, had grounded here. Most of the victims of Flint's, though, as of the other hazards along the Ohio's thousand-mile course, were family boats, manned by immigrants knowing little of the river's ways and used only to guiding mules over a rutted path, if so much as that. Deluded by the river's apparent tranquillity, unused to

95

chutes and ripples, they embarked with visions of being wafted gently down to their destination by the smooth, unruffled current of La Belle Rivière. Most awakened roughly to reality at Dead Man's Ripple, just below Pittsburgh, or at like spots below their starting point, and thereafter kept the *Navigator* open for future reference. Even with its guidance, because channels changed and snags proliferated and deadly fogs came drifting in and floating ice trapped the unwary (none traveled when the great towering floes built up), many a neophyte navigator ran afoul of the river's traps, and soon another wreck—of a boat, a family, of a long-held dream, was added to the river's toll.

But the *New Orleans* was ahead of the ice by weeks and Andrew Jack was no neophyte. Lydia, standing at the bow to watch him maneuver through the channel—hugging an island, pulling out quickly to avoid a sandbar, judging the strength of a ripple and finding the chute—marveled at his skill. In the engine room, the hands kept the firebox filled under Baker's supervision, and the *New Orleans,* paddle wheels churning and smoke billowing, moved proudly down the reaches of the river and around the bends. Nicholas, Lydia observed, moved just as proudly, pacing here and there, checking the charts and the progress points. There was an affinity between man and boat, more than just a relationship between a thing built and the builder. The *New Orleans* was a projection of her maker's spirit; her pulse beat with his.

It was a pulse repeated in the unanimity of effort as the crew went about their duties. Used to action, to demands on their skills and their muscles, they had regained their earlier zest; the glum talk heard in the taverns was forgotten as they contemplated happily the high pay that would be theirs on the completion of the voyage. Mr. Roosevelt was not one to be niggardly when bountiful recompense would insure the effort he sought, especially when the money to be paid was not his own. It was reflected, too, in Lydia's own buoyant mood, and even the children seemed happier. Everyone seemed determined to triumph over the continuing surliness of the weather, to shake off the heaviness that hung around them.

And there was so much to see! Honking V's of geese passing high in the misty sky in the morning and late afternoon, soaring eagles, thousands and thousands of blackbirds crossing above ("Birdie!" Rosetta cried, clapping her hands), and once at twilight several flocks of trumpeter swans, snowy and elegant, flying from different directions toward a hidden lake, their magnificent wings spreading ten feet across from tip to tip. So had John James Audubon described them as he saw them one winter morning only the year before, near the mouth of the Ohio. He had seen the sight of their rising, too, seen them start from the ice-bound river with wings extended as if in some wild race, the pattering of their feet sounding like the noise of great muffled drums and their loud, clear calls filling the air, then rise as one in a vision of beauty after the run to windward that brought all of them on the wing.

Flocks of pelicans flew over, too, migrating southward, and on the second day came the passenger pigeons, darkening the sky, flock after flock wheeling and darting, one following the pattern set by another as it swooped and rose to escape the following hawks. The beat of their wings could be heard even above the steamboat's rumble; it was a continuous roar as they swept over by the thousands, the hundreds of thousands, and into the forest; it was audible three miles away to the farmers, the hunters, the wolves and foxes and bears. Pigs would be led to fatten on their corpses, the settlers around would eat pigeon for weeks, and when they left the forest, the place where they had been would be as devastated as if a tornado had passed through. Lydia counted the flocks up to a hundred, then gave up. They could keep coming for days.

On the river too were other sights, man-made: the barges loaded with barrels of flour and whisky and grain; the sleek keel-boats; the family boats, on which astonished travelers stared at the steamboat as it passed—and coming toward them once a keelboat of some forty tons working its way upriver by means of a horizontal wheel kept in motion by six horses going around in a circle on a gallery above the boat. Even Nicholas, attracted as always by any device that made things move, could not resist taking a moment to watch despite his familiarity with the contraption. Two cog wheels were fixed each to an axle projecting over the gunwale, one forward and one aft of the wheel, and eight paddles fixed to the projecting end of each axle moved the boat forward.

They passed a floating gristmill beside the bank that was made up of a large scow supporting one end of the shaft of a waterwheel as well as the stones and gears, and two other vessels, one a canoe to hold the other end of the wheel, and one for the waiting grain. The rushing current obligingly turned the waterwheel, and the entire mill was fastened by grapevine rope to a tree that leaned out from the shore. The two little boys who ran it came rushing over to watch the steamboat pass, and waved. Nicholas, goodhumoredly waving back, remarked that turn about was fair enough: when *he* was a boy, it was just such machinery as that gristmill that had given him the vision of the paddle wheels they traveled on now.

There were other sights, less happy ones—a flatboat overturned, a broken chair floating ludicrously upright as though waiting for an occupant, a jacket caught on a jagged stump, those signs seen every season along the rivers of ruin or abandonment, wrecked vessels, even sometimes the glimpse of a floating body, and graves, graves, so many of them the Lilliputian ones remarked on by travelers. Many children were born, but many were buried, too. For a moment, hugging Rosetta to her, Lydia's high spirits flagged; the feeling of contentment was ruffled by a chill of foreboding. A wind had sprung up, relieving somewhat the heavy stillness of the air, but threatening to make the passage the rest of the way more hazardous, raising the white caps that had given the river its name, *Ohio,* not "beautiful," as the French had believed, but a part of the Miama word *Ohiopeekhanne,* "the white foaming river." Indeed, the French to whom the Ohio was La Belle Rivière had given it its name when they were seeing the upper waters now called the Allegheny, limpid and smooth; in those early times there was no thought that the Ohio was formed by the junction of that glittering river with the muddy Monongahela.

River scene showing a flatboat and two keelboats.

In late afternoon, they stopped at a small settlement where they had been hospitably received on the flatboat trip. Lydia remembered buying some fine fat turkeys there from a farmer's wife, along with milk and eggs; they could use some again. Nicholas thought it a good idea to take on more wood, even though Yellow Bank lay not far ahead, and all aboard would welcome a time ashore. Henry, she decided, who was comfortably full and sleepy, could be left on board with the maids, and she and Rosetta could have an excursion on their own.

The little group of houses, some dozen or so, on the shore of a creek, were more than had been there two years earlier, but no one was surprised. In this region, no settlement stood still. Either those who had set down roots found the going too hard and let their hopes wither and die, or the evidence of their flourishing farms brought others to clear and plant and pursue their dreams in so likely a place. This one, close by the mouth of a wide creek, a convenient stop for passing boats to take on provisions or to shelter for the night, could prosper as others had. The pattern was already set in this rich, promising land. A settlement of small farms would appear. An enterprising pioneer 99 would set up a general store. Soon a small mill would be built, then a smithy. The village could become a town, with brick houses, a tavern or two, a post office, perhaps a courthouse and jail. And a town—who knew? By virtue of location or good fortune or special enterprise, a town could become in time a city of consequence, where a small group of pioneers like these, who had come to a wilderness with little thought of history but with much courage and hope, would be venerated by later generations as its founders.

The group that approached as the mooring line was tied to a tree on the bank looked hardly venerable, however. A few men, dressed in a motley combination of homespun and buckskin, two young pregnant women in linen sunbonnets and linsey-woolsey dresses and makeshift jackets, with woolen stockings and homemade shoes, and another of indeterminate age, gaunt and weary, appeared, all of them missing at least two teeth. There were children of all sizes; after their first wary hesitation they advanced toward Rosetta, who looked like a miniature lady in her long skirt and the little fur-trimmed cape that Lydia had put on her against the December chill.

Leading her by the hand, Lydia hurried toward the older woman. Did she remember her? she asked. She had come down here in a flatboat the summer before last and bought three turkeys and a hen. The woman professed dourly that she "mought." Like most frontier women, she was not garrulous with strangers, especially possible Yankees, with their wooden nutmegs; it was the frontier men who had established the American reputation for inquisitiveness. Most of the time, the women simply did the work that visitors entailed. But as her own toddler moved over toward the little girl, she smiled briefly and acknowledged as how she had some middlin' to fair turkeys—and was the lady interested in eggs and butter? She could not keep her eyes from the steamboat, looking at her a little fearfully. Yes, they'd all heard tell about it, she said in answer to Lydia's question. The rivermen who stopped had few kind words for it, either; they said it would bring bad luck along the river, and speaking honest, there warn't no two ways about it—some skeery things had been a-happening. For a moment a superstitious fear showed in her widened eyes, and then she turned briskly to business. Turkeys were twenty-five cents for the smallest, fifty cents for the large; eggs and milk could be had at six and a quarter cents for a dozen of the one, the same for a quart of the other. Lydia agreed on the price, and the woman motioned to the boys and the black servant who stood over by the house to get started.

Get started they did. With a shout and a whoop, the boys descended upon the poultry yard in back of the house, the dogs yelped furiously, and the turkeys, with a flurry of wings and wild squawking, ran for the shelter of the henhouse, which was raised upon logs. The woman joined in then, standing in front of them as they came, and moved with surprising agility from side to side, shooing them back with her skirts spread wide. Clearly she enjoyed the chase as much as the children did. A turkey scooted past her, made a lunge underneath the house, and the dog, with delighted growls and barks, bellied down to wriggle under the shelter and chase the bird out on the other side into the arms of one of the boys. It was a wonderful game. Rosetta clapped her hands and pulled at Lydia's skirts to bring her closer as the woman picked up an axe and stood waiting at the chopping block. She knew the funniest part would come after, when the birds went running around with their heads cut off. Lydia, laughing, brought her over—theirs was not an age of squeamishness—and stood talking to the woman, who was, she said, from Virginny. Her man had gotten tired of scrabbling and they'd come over the Cumberland Road three years gone and taken boat at Marietta. This here place had seemed a likely one; she'd had three babies since. As the birds' heads dropped off and the headless creatures ran around in their death throes, Rosetta took the corn given her and fed it to the clucking hens that gathered, oblivious to the grim omen of their future fate.

Aboard once again, Rosetta ran over to Tiger, who waited patiently at the head of the plank, and laughed in delight as he sniffed suspiciously at the turkey scent she brought back with her. Lydia stopped dutifully to pat the big head; it was she whom Tiger worshipped, and it was beside her that he settled whenever there was a choice. Taking little Henry from the nurse's arms, she retired to the cabin to nurse him, feeling a sweet contentment in the process, contentment, too, in the feeling of relief as she loosened her stays, in the steady progress they were making, in the supply of provisions planned to take care of them all the way to Natchez, in the warmth of their reception all along the way. As she put Henry down, swaddled and happy, she stood over him for a moment, just looking. Where would he go? What would he do? What kind of man would he be? Surely a child born on the first steamboat to challenge the western waters was linked mysteriously to the future of this opening land. What would it mean to him? He to it? How frightening, how exciting, was the thought of the future stretching so far ahead! For this land. For her son.

They put in for the night at a small willow island near a creek, the roar of the fire in the furnace dying away, the paddle wheels slowing, sparks from the chimney floating, dancing upward, toward the comet that was not yet visible, that might not be visible this night, hidden as it was in the murky sky. Those who were watching from the forest murmured, their voices troubled and angry. Fire. Fire in the sky. Fire on the river. *Penelore,* the Fire Canoe. What were the spirits saying?

On board the *New Orleans,* too, there was talk of the comet. Here in the night, with the howling of wolves echoing from the darkness, with the hooting of owls and the eerie night cry of panthers and the shrieks of small animals caught by predators, even the distant baying of a settler's hounds increased the sense that the brooding atmosphere held the vessel in some mysterious spell. So much had the comet become a part of everyone's consciousness that even its nonappearance caused concern, and some of the crew remembered hearing that when a comet left, it was because the disaster it portended was at hand. Andrew Jack's bluff scoffing reassured them somewhat; he was respected for his cool head and self-confidence as well as for his skills, and the murmurings gradually died away.

Despite the disturbing noises and the imagined omens, the night passed without incident. Dawn brought all hands awake, the cook to his fire and Baker to his, and the steamboat set out for Yellow Bank, not far downriver now.

The shores were lowering steadily. Hanging Rock was visible ahead, that bare, perpendicular bluff of solid rock, a hundred feet high, that stood like a period marking the end of the hill country. Cane brakes, great thickets of evergreen that grew ten to twelve feet high and that sheltered and fed cattle all winter for farmers—but harbored, unfortunately for the cattle, bears as well—were beginning to show, and here and there groves of tall cottonwood trees, leafless now, lined the shore. In their branches clusters of glossy mistletoe hung, the white berries looking like snowdrops against the leaves. The skeletal December look of the trees against a sombre sky gave a chill to the atmosphere. There was a chill in the air, too, not a brisk, enlivening one but raw and penetrating. Vultures wheeled with deceptive laziness in the sky, searching hungrily for the dying and the dead. Bare vines writhed and clung to the high limbs of the trees, making a pattern almost like writing, Lydia thought, as though they penned a message: The season of sorrow is at hand. She shivered. What made her think this way? Was it because December had not brought the clearing winds one had a right to expect? Where was the bright touch of frost? Or the cleansing purge of a thunderstorm? The misty, cloudless sky, the bare, ravaged trees, the earth where the dry grass rustled, all seemed to be waiting, waiting. Even the river had nothing to say. Taking them silently toward the west, toward what was to be, it seemed eager to be done with them.

By late afternoon, though, as they neared Yellow Bank, the bustle of preparation for landing enlivened the world once more. They would stay here overnight, for there would be a good day's work in digging the coal and gathering it aboard. The banks of the river began to show the yellow, sulphurous cast, strangely like that of the sky, that had given the region its name, and as dusk was falling they reached Island Sixty-eight, so marked in the *Navigator,* which lay close to the right shore, the Indiana shore, five miles above Yellow Bank itself and just opposite the site of the mine on the Indiana side. As darkness fell, Jack guided

103

the *New Orleans* to her landing at the foot of the island, where she would be protected from driftwood and whatever else might come downriver in the night.

Again no stars showed.

They woke to a misty dawn, and astonishment. At the site of the mine a great pile of coal, already quarried, lay there for the taking. Crewmen scheduled to go ashore to begin the digging muttered uneasily, moving about on the deck. Who the heck—? How—? There were too many funny things happening! They looked toward Nicholas.

Poachers, of course! Angrily he pointed toward a trail of spilled coal leading down to the water's edge where the mark of a loading plank was visible. How much had been dug out in the year past? How much had gone downriver to be sold to the settlers or to the Natchez blacksmiths who were always eager for the harder coal from upriver? No mere settlers would have taken the trouble to dig the coal with all the wood for fuel at hand for the cutting. Someone else was making a profit on his mines. Well, the thieves would find this load gone when they returned!

"Load up!" he ordered; and the crewmen, delighted to see much of their work already done, paraded down the plank with pickaxes and shovels. At least half of what the *New Orleans* could accommodate was in the piles, and Nicholas revised his estimate of when they could be on their way. With all the loading finished by that night, as now seemed possible, they could leave at dawn.

For Lydia, a whole day ashore with no rain in sight was too inviting to resist. The cabin was comfortable, the boat large, and the scenery wonderfully interesting, but, oh, how nice to enjoy the earth! In those woods along the Ohio, there was little underbrush even in the growing season, so effectively did the great canopies of grapevines exclude the sunlight, and there were clearings always at hand for picnicking or strolling. This side of the river was largely uninhabited, at least by settlers, but they would have Tiger to guard them and the ready rifles of the crew for protection against the ever-present if remote possibility of bears or even of the wild hogs that could be bold and mean. And if that need did not arise, the guns would still be useful; pheasant and rabbit and squirrel were always welcome supplements to the daily fare.

Lydia happily ordered sandwiches from the cook, of sliced turkey and duck. Sandwiches were a wonderful innovation introduced not many years earlier; it was said that they were invented by, or for, the Earl of Sandwich, who refused to leave the gambling table to eat a proper meal. Nicholas only nodded as they left; he was distracted, still incensed at the effrontery of the poachers and trying to figure out a way to put a stop to their depredations.

They were having a lovely time, Rosetta picking up brown leaves here and there to bring triumphantly to her mother. "Leaf, leaf," she would say each time. "Mama hold." She was saying so many words, putting them together now. Henry lay happily on Nanny's lap, his blue eyes contentedly following the movement of stray leaves above or a darting parakeet. It was with some alarm that Lydia looked up from the circle they had formed in the clearing under a grove of beeches to see Tiger's sudden stance of warning, ruff standing up on his neck, a growl rumbling deep in his throat. "Stay!" she ordered in a low tone, getting up quickly to put her hand on his collar. Two of the men working the coal saw her movement and reached quickly for their rifles, and Rosetta, at her mother's sharp command, flew to hide behind her skirts. One of the men came toward them quickly; the other waited, rifle ready. Nicholas was still aboard.

There were voices, and Lydia relaxed. Indians would not speak. In a moment she saw a group of people emerging slowly and hesitantly from the woods, in which, she realized as she noticed a wisp of smoke rising in the distance, there must be dwellings. These visitors were a shabby lot. Squatters. Some of that unsavory tribe that drifted along on the edge of the great movement to the West, living in squalor and moving on when the settlers—the substantial, ambitious immigrants—moved in. Occasionally, rarely, some of them took root and from their planting good stock grew. But not often.

Panicking for a moment, Lydia had visions of a great swarm of hungry squatters descending upon them and demanding all   *105* their stores. Then she saw that they were carrying their belongings and that the children were strangely silent, as though cowed by some general fear. Could it be that they were survivors of an Indian attack? All her old fears rising, she looked wildly around and saw with relief that the children were safely on their way to the boarding plank with the two maids, who had picked them up at once and started for the steamboat, and then she saw one of the crew walking over to talk to the visitors.

One of the men in the approaching group took over as spokesman; she could see him motioning toward the steamboat, asking questions. Others joined in then, as though they could not wait for the answers. She herself was questioning, too. Where was Nicholas? Where *was* he? And then she saw him running down the plank, taking a quick look to assure himself that she was safe, and going toward the group with a stern expression on his face. He could not possibly be thinking that these people were the poachers; the poor, straggling things wouldn't have had the strength to dig the coal! Impatient and curious, she wished that she too could join them, but feeling Tiger's quivering eagerness to attack, his barely restrained hostility, she dared not let him go. Soon she saw Nicholas shrug, looking annoyed, and turn to come toward her. It seemed, he said, that the squatters had stopped talking when he arrived on the scene; evidently they found him intimidating. Even in her anxiety, she had to smile; she could imagine the effect Nicholas's brusque and commanding approach had had on these isolated, suspicious people. For of course he would have asked them about the coal, and probably none too gently. Discreetly, she said nothing. They waited.

At last the two crewmen came over to report, shaking their heads in mock wonder and making whirling motions with their fingers at their temples, laughing. These folk hereabouts must have been going to too many camp meetings, they said. They were already scared of their own shadows, with the comet and all, and when the steamboat came along, smoking and rumbling and splashing, they got in a terrible dither, figured she was a devil ship or something. They were asking if her wheels made the ground shake, made it rumble, all of them a-swearing they could feel it. Nicholas frowned. Much as he enjoyed creating a sensation, he wanted no hostility toward the steamboat, especially out here, but there was no way of reassuring these people. Certainly he could not invite them aboard. With a wave of his hand, he dismissed the whole incident and told the men to get back to work. As Lydia watched, the group begin to straggle away uncertainly into the woods, looking back with anxious faces. They seemed to her more pathetic than mean or ridiculous and she wondered if perhaps a reassuring word would help. Impulsively she started toward them—and stopped after the first step. Such hostility showed in their faces as they stared resentfully back at her that it was clear she too was held to blame for whatever it was they feared.

The coal was finally aboard, but Nicholas decided that little time could be gained by departing that night. The going then was always slow, because even if sandbars and shoals were not a danger, darkness hid the dangerous eddies that formed in the river's bends, and there was always the danger that the steamboat's speed could bring her hurtling mercilessly down upon some hapless vessel floating with the stream. What terror for a flatboat's occupants!—to see this monstrous, fiery apparition bearing down upon them from around a bend with no chance, no hope of stopping its advance. No, they would depart at dawn and stop next evening at Henderson, some eighty miles beyond. There they would see old friends, mail letters, even perhaps— Nicholas's hopes never flagged—gain some new subscribers to the Ohio Steamboat Navigation Company and even persuade some farsighted merchants to risk their cargoes aboard the *New Orleans.*

And then, the second day after that, they should reach the big river, the Mississippi, the one that mattered. Let those who would claim that the Missouri was the main stream, the Mississippi its branch; let the explorers continue to search for its still unknown source—all these things mattered little. What did matter was that some day the nation would reach across that great crooked river that now effectively blocked settlement. And because trade was the lifeblood of nations and that stream the main artery through which the blood of the nation must flow, whoever tapped well into it would have his fortune made. One of the first to do so, if everything went as planned, would be Nicholas I. Roosevelt, of Pittsburgh and New York.

By the time all the coal was stowed and the boat in order once again, with time taken for the interruption caused by the terrified squatters, the sun was lowering behind the distant tree-tops, its dull, coppery glow still visible through the spidery sculpture of their branches, descending toward the mighty, brooding river that waited to the west. Lydia, still unnerved by the encounter with the squatters and disconcerted by their unexpected hostility, had lost the feeling of exhilaration that she had brought with her to the forest clearing. As she sat in the cabin holding Henry in her arms, she leaned down and kissed the top of his head—softer than eiderdown, the wispy hair!—and wondered if she had been right to insist on coming, on bringing her children on this long, strange voyage. Perhaps she and they, at least, should have stayed in Louisville. But even as she wondered, she knew that she was only torturing her conscience from a sense of duty. She could not have *stood* being so long without Nicholas, and he needed—she knew it better than he did—her faith, her confidence, her need of him to pursue the task ahead.

Brushing off her apprehension as mere moodiness (Nicholas accepted her moods as an aspect of femaleness and never paid much attention to them anyway), she looked up and smiled as he entered the cabin and came over to kiss her and the baby and then Rosetta, who was sound asleep. He was relieved, he said. He'd written the blasted report to Fulton to be posted at Henderson, and wouldn't write another until they reached Natchez. What was the point of writing a whole lot of useless detail that would be entered in the ship's log and in his account books anyway? Stretching and yawning, he seemed content; the poachers were evidently forgotten. The steamboat was going along splendidly, wasn't she? There were a few changes he'd make in the engine for the next boat, but not many. Wait until the people in Henderson saw her! Remember, Lyd, how sure they were we'd never make it? How about inviting Audubon's friend Dr. Rankin

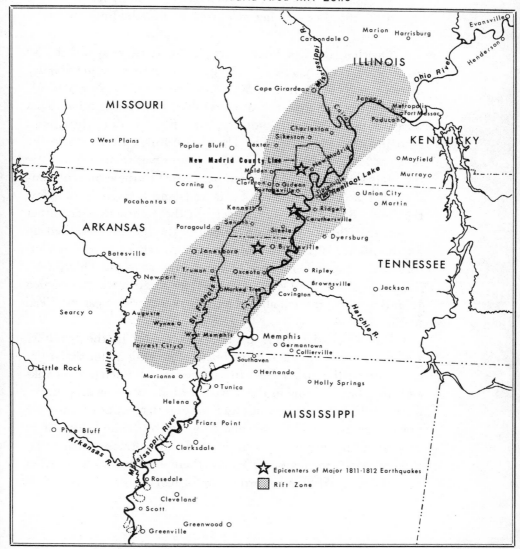

MICHAEL NEWTON SAMSOT

aboard with his family for a little visit? How many children did he have? Thirteen? He laughed, wondered if he and Lydia would do as well.

So jubilant was he, so full of plans, that Lydia could not bear to let him know of her own feeling of foreboding.

On that night of December 15, 1811, they lay about 250 miles from their meeting with the wicked river, some seventy more from New Madrid, in Missouri Territory. In New Madrid, that night of the fifteenth of December, the French inhabitants were having a "frolick"; others, like Eliza Bryan, the young schoolmistress, lay sleeping. Thirty-two miles farther down the river, at Little Prairie, elderly Mrs. Lafont was tossing restlessly; the nights were long. Her thoughts turned to the emigrant families that had moored their boats at Island Sixteen, just below the town. Still farther downriver, on the Kentucky side, other vessels traveling in company for fear of the Indians were tied up for the night. William Leigh Pierce, a merchant from Philadelphia, was a passenger on one of them. And at Island Thirty-five, five miles above the Devil's Channel, an English traveler named John Bradbury traveled aboard a barge that carried a cargo of lead to Natchez.

All along the river, up and down, and in the tributary streams, family boats and cargo boats were tying up for this night that seemed like any other. In villages that bordered the banks and in isolated cabins in the woods, in Indian towns deep in the forest and along the meandering bayous that emptied into the great river, men and women and children, birds and beasts, slept or coupled or hunted or were hunted, all of them waiting, although they did not know it, for their meeting with an event that had been coming toward them for half a billion years.

7

Deep in the North American continent, four miles beneath the surface of the earth, a hard rock trough with walls two miles high extends for a hundred and twenty miles beneath the Mississippi Valley floor. It is thirty miles wide and about six hundred million years old and is there because one day a crack formed in the continental plate floating on the earth's thick crust. In the mantle that encloses the deep hot recesses of the earth, molten rock discovered the crack, came seeping tentatively forth into the brighter world, became a trickle, then a flow, and finally a gushing eruption—masses of material from inner earth welling forth onto what was then its surface.

The flow ceased. Why, no one knows, any more than why it began. But the rift remained. Within it, over uncounted millions of years, the molten matter hardened, became rock; over it accumulated the debris of great geologic events, the abrasive residue of ponderous rocky encounters, soil and dust particles blown by primeval winds or carried along streams long gone, clay and sand gravel pushed into it by glacial drift, marine deposits from shallow covering seas, even the dust of meteorites. Finally, *111* before any eyes were there to see it, four miles of sediment hid it from view.

The molten matter, hardening into layers of rock within the rift, had its own history. At first the layers lay symmetrically in place. Then, some hundred million years ago, or more, or less, about a mile below what had become the surface, something happened to disturb their symmetry, a volcano, perhaps, or a shift in the solidity of what lay beneath. A layer sank, or another was uplifted in some mysterious upheaval, and within the rift a fault, itself three thousand feet deep, was created. Along a large crack, corresponding layers of rock were offset vertically, in some places by as much as thirty-three hundred feet. As the North American plate moves slowly, slowly, squeezing just a little the area of the rift, the layers of rock within it grind uncomfortably against one another, pushing for place. The tension can become intolerable.

In late Tertiary time, several million years ago, the sea that covered much of the land that would be North America receded, and what had been its bed rose to become a coastal plain over which a young river, which had been of modest length, began reaching grandly to the gulf that lay far to the south. With the extension, it gained stature, drew to itself other rivers, exacting from them complete subservience and all their waters. Fiercely it cut its way along the plain, and at last, by means of a system that embraced more than a million and a quarter square miles, drained one-eighth of the North American continent, an area as great as England and Wales and Scotland, France and Spain and Portugal, Germany, Austria, Italy, and Turkey combined. It carried to the gulf below some seven hundred and twenty-four billion cubic feet of water every year, and within that water a half billion tons of rich alluvial mud. Later, in an industrial age, its burden would be less rich, more deadly.

It was an arrogant river, choosing its own path, taking its time. Along part of the four-thousand-mile course it formed with its great tributary, the Missouri, it used thirteen hundred miles to cover the same ground that a crow would fly over—if a crow were interested and able—in six hundred and seventy-five. When it found its banks oppressive, it cut through them, pushing sideways or across, leaving parts of its former bed to become dry land, making islands of what had been river bank and jutting points, moving a forest from one side of itself to another, splitting islands in two, rushing in sudden impulse down cypress-bound chutes to form new channels, letting the old ones be silted in. When white men finally discovered this river, and, after a century and a half of astonishing indifference, began to explore it, when flatboats and keelboats and barges joined the bark canoes that had been traversing it for centuries, it maintained its lordly ways, continuing to treat the land cavalierly, the humans, in their absurd and fragile vessels, with lofty disdain. About it superstitions grew: Rivermen knew of phantom vessels, with their moaning crews, caught forever in chutes dead-ended by the river's moods, of boats that passed in the night with a fox-fire glow about them and no crew to be seen. Indians feared the demon who dwelt in the river's depths and whose roar could be heard in the angry voice of the waters as they rushed through the branches of toppled trees. But no one suggested that *beneath* those depths a demon might have its abode.

In the earth's long history, lost among a million cataclysms, the movement was a mere shrug.

With a crash, a cracking, a thunderous roar, heaving and tearing, the earth convulsed. In the Mississippi Valley, from upper Canada to the Gulf, in an area fifty thousand miles square, the shocks began. In the early morning hours of December 16, up and down the river, at Little Prairie, at New Madrid, in Indian towns and white men's villages, in vessels tied up along the way or floating along the stream, fulfilling the preachers' prophecies of doom, the terror came.

It found the frolickers at New Madrid, roused the sleepers—Eliza Bryan, seventeen, and her neighbor, Mrs. Gray, who loved Plato and had all his works; the Protestant minister and the Catholic priest; the judge and Mr. Belson, the keeper of pigs, woke all of the four hundred families in town to an "awful darkness" and a sulphurous, choking mist. They heard the rumble of thunder deep in the earth and the crash of chimneys, felt the *113* floors beneath them sway and rock. Clutching at bedsteads and sills, crying and calling, they fled from their tumbling houses, save those who could not, like teenage Betsy Masters, pinned in her bed by the roof pole and whimpering with the pain of a broken leg. In a darkness ripped every few minutes by angry blue flashes they saw their neighbors running and falling, running again as they reached out, sobbing, shouting. Is my child here? My wife? What—? Where—? Their voices were part of a terrible moan that was made up of underground thunder and the river's roar, of the cracking and sighing of trees, of the staccato, explo-

A woodcut of the great earthquake at New Madrid. From *Historical Collections of the Great West* by Henry Howe, 1857.

sive sounds made by a vomiting earth and the evil hiss of gases jetting toward the sky, of the lowing of cattle and the screams of birds and the cries of forest creatures wakened in the night. There in the open, praying together now, Catholic and Protestant, who had never prayed together before, felt the earth—*saw* it!—rising and falling in waves several feet high like the waves of the sea, waves that threw them off their feet, saw them burst and send forth streams of water and sand and black bituminous shale.

Rivermen sleeping aboard their boats at the foot of Chepousa Creek just above town awoke to the surge of rushing waters roaring in, lifting them, pushing, lifting them again, higher, higher on the crest of an enormous wave that carried them (how long? forever!) back, back, and then, if their vessels were not swept out with its ebb, dropping them sickeningly on the sand, along with gasping, flopping fish and fragments of smashed boats and slimy debris cast up from the river's depths. They leaped out from their rocking boats and scrambled frantically in the eerie, flash-lit darkness, some one way, some another, running to reach land beyond the river's reach, if such there was. In the flashes of light they saw downstream a mountain of water rising against a barrier that had not been there before, saw it climb higher and higher, a monstrous thing of water that must fall back, had to fall back, upon itself. But none of them waited to see as behind them the wave continued to rise against the barrier while the river writhed in torment, buffeted by that force beneath its bed, until the wave and then the river itself, betrayed by a nature in disorder, fell back, reversed direction—and flowed upstream.

There remained for silent witness to this monstrous violation of natural law, this cosmic insult, a grove of cottonwood and willow trees two and a half miles long all stripped of leaves and branches, bent upstream.

All night the townspeople huddled together, while fissures opened beneath their feet and from yawning holes spouted jets of warm water and sand and pit coal that flew as high as the tops of trees. In the morning they would see, on their earth, the mas- 115 sive bones of a creature that had died some thirty thousand years before. There was no escaping to the hills twenty-five miles away. Where the plain had been, around which New Madrid was built, a lake stretched twenty miles across; lakes farther off had become bare land. As they saw in glimpses the bluffs beyond the town, bluffs that had been of a height with their own, they saw that the town itself had fallen and they with it, along with houses and barns. One of the huddled group, a woman, died of fright while shock succeeded shock, and the people of New Madrid, scholar and dunce and old and young, rowdy rivermen and Mrs. Gray, French and English and Spanish, prayed and awaited the dawn.

But the dawn was no dawn. It was a purplish, sulphur-tainted haze that showed tall trees waving like the spars of a ship in a storm, with no storm, some of them lashed together in tangled protest, bending this way and that, tossing their arms about wildly in a gesture of despair. Terrified birds flew aimlessly, directionless, and found rest on the heads of even more terrified humans, old fears forgotten in the new. Horses stamped and neighed in wild terror, calves bawled, dogs howled. The light showed the graveyard thrown into the bend of the river and bodies floating or scattered about, and how many were old and how many new it was impossible to know, so many were the wrecks on the river. Daylight brought some measure of calm, so that there were those who noticed that the fissures that ripped across the land formed in parallel lines, southwest to northeast, with intervals of half a mile between; if they could fell trees at right angles to the chasms they could be safe upon them even as the earth opened below. It was a wild hope, an impossible thought at first, but in the coming days it would save them, most of them. But now they could only wait for the shaking, rocking world to be still. They would wait for months.

Betsy Masters was lucky. Thirty miles to the north Colonel John Shaw, of Marquette County, Wisconsin, hurried toward New Madrid when daylight came. He would free her from her prison, tend the injured leg.

At Little Prairie, thirty miles downriver, Godfrey Le Sieur, son of the town's founder, stumbling like his fellows in the eerie darkness, reaching now here, now there to give support or seek it, felt the night imprinted forever on his mind. He knew that the town itself, still fragile, hardly a generation old, must die of a shock so great. As indeed it did. But Le Sieur told later the tale of its passing, of the cries of Little Prairie's hundred families as the earth beneath them was ripped apart, and of the empty flatboats on the river, telling their own story, of barrels of flour and pork and whisky floating on a river where those whose cargo they were had disappeared. He told of the Glasscock family, six or eight in number, who had moored their vessel at Island Sixteen, just below Little Prairie, and who were never seen again; of the man from Tennessee, who was discovered floating on a plank and rescued, almost mad from the memory of his lost wife and seven children as well as the young man traveling with them to the West, where life was going to be splendid and land was free. We know from Le Sieur of Mrs. Jarvis, who rushed from her bed as her cabin fell about her and was struck by a log, to lie helpless for three days until she died, and of her neighbor, Mrs. Lafont, who felt the terror like a knife and died as suddenly as if it had been. He did not tell us if they were young or old or if they too loved Plato. Did they leave husbands and children to mourn them? Who came to help? Could anyone help anyone else with the world breaking apart?

One of the travelers on the river that fateful night was William Leigh Pierce, on his way from Pittsburgh to New Orleans, who entered the Mississippi on Friday the thirteenth. He it was who was traveling in company, as were a number of others, "the more effectively to guard against anticipated attacks from the Savage, who are said to be at present much exasperated against the whites." On that night of December fifteenth, the night of events predetermined by those ancient happenings, all the vessels in his company were moored some miles below Little Prairie, on the Kentucky side of the river. It had been an overcast day, heavy and oppressive; the night was still and starless, and some of the travelers, caught willy-nilly like so many others in the comet's spell, wondered about it. Had it gone into the far reaches of *117* space? (Space was just space then; no one thought of it as a place for people to go.) Or was it still there, behind the obscuring haze, riding the distant sky? Was it true that comets appeared before catastrophes? That a comet had caused the Deluge? Or at least foretold it? Some of the passengers, like Pierce, were well-informed men, speculative; some of those in the company could not read or write, and in the conversation was the curious mix of intelligent speculation and popular superstition that heavenly bodies have ever provoked.

The crews had their nightly ration of whisky, always a generous one, but out on the river their thirst was less prodigious than in town and most of them, along with Pierce, were sleeping at 2:00 A.M.

It was then that it came, at 2:00 A.M. Everyone agreed on that—the unearthly noise, the wild agitation of the boats, a sound like the sound of artillery fire tearing the night apart, the terror—

Indians! They had loosed the cables! They were attacking from shore! Were gathering in the river! The men seized rifles and knives and rushed out on deck, looking wildly about where not even shadows could be seen; they ran together body into body and came perilously close to killing one another in the dark. But even as they met, swearing and shouting, the vessels were again convulsed and a nearby oak tree cracked in two, its mighty trunk, limbs waving, falling into the nearby waters and stirring them into a giant wave—and all in the company knew that not even Indians had such power.

They milled about then, calling from boat to boat in voices hoarse with fear, cried out, prayed. Let's go! Where? Where? We can't stay here! The boats'll be smashed! Can't go—the river's full of trees! From the woods around, from the islands, from the river's banks, rose the screams of swans and geese and ducks as they were startled into flight. The raucous, shrill noises filled the night and only flashes of blue from sulphurous gases jetting upward lighted the way ahead. It was impossible to go on.

At dawn, in a purplish demonic light, the travelers saw the river, an unbelievable river, churning and roiling, its color reddish, as though tinged with blood, and thick with mud and foam. Here and there were upturned canoes and flatboats floating empty or caught in the branches of trees that had hurtled into the air, some from depths where they had lain for centuries, only to fall back into the stream.

Now they saw that the sound like artillery fire, which they had thought was caused by the falling in of the banks, came rather from the jetting, hissing discharges exploding from funnellike holes in the earth, spilling all around them water as warm as if heated and sand and sticks and lumps of coal, all of them shooting up thirty feet or more into the murky air. The rumbling under the earth was incessant, fissures were forming as the earth waves broke on the nearby shore, and all agreed that to move on now that daylight, such as it was, had come would be safer than to stay. Hardly had they pulled away, at seven o'clock in the morning—another precise detail that would be remembered—when there came another shock as violent as the first, and the bank they had just abandoned collapsed into the flood.

All day the shocks continued, with hardly an interval between them. All day the pilots steered their vessels around the thousands of trees torn from shore or thrown up from the river bottom to become great snags, planters that seemed to be growing in the river, sometimes upside down, or deadly sawyers, waving their branches mockingly before them. The air was sulphurous, the water tainted with its smell, the sky still brooding. They found a sort of refuge, finally, at a willow island, and anchored there. Next day there were some who took courage, with the shocks perceptible but lessening, to explore the island to see what damage had been done. They found frightful caverns and burnt wood in every stage, from kindling to coal, found holes in the earth, one sixteen feet deep and sixty-three feet across, with lumps of coal fifteen or twenty pounds in weight scattered around as far as one hundred and sixty measured paces from its gaping mouth. They found the corpses of birds and small animals that lived on the river island; those that survived were immobilized with fright.

On the nineteenth of December, William Leigh Pierce and 119

The Mississippi River during the 1811–1812 earthquakes, as shown in a nine-teenth-century book. Courtesy of the State Historical Society of Missouri.

his company loosed the cables and resumed their downstream path. At Long Reach, one hundred and forty-six miles beyond the mouth of the Ohio, the trees that blocked their passage made a continuous forest growing from the river bed. Everywhere such forests rose above the surface, and everywhere could be seen thousands of acres of what had been forest now flooded by waters that spread like a sea across the land. They passed Fort Pickering, just below Wolf River, and saw the blockhouse tremble. But at last on Christmas Eve, after two hundred terrible miles, they moored at the mouth of the St. Francis River, in Louisiana Territory, a meeting place for hunters and traders from the West and a depository for their fur goods and peltries. Next day, from nearby Big Prairie, Pierce—a man not easily rattled!—wrote calmly of what had happened in a letter to the *New York Evening World*. To his vivid description he added a surmise:

> The many and repeated shocks of Earthquakes which have been felt in our southern and southwestern States, indicate that there has been some terrible, and perhaps destructive eruption of the Earth, somewhere to the south-west of us, perhaps Mexico, New-Spain, or Quito, of which we are hereafter to have tidings.

Those tidings came, months later. While the terror continued at New Madrid, on a night when the earth still trembled and the comet was again visible, along with flashing lights and an extraordinary rumbling of subterranean thunder, the town of Caracas, in newly independent Venezuela, was destroyed, its ten thousand inhabitants buried in the rubble of stone houses tumbled by a terrible quake, while from beneath the llanos of the surrounding region and even out at sea the angry rumbling rose.

On the night that Pierce and his company moored their boats at Little Prairie, an Englishman named John Bradbury, a mineralogist and botanist traveling in America, as was the fashion for those interested in the exotic, was on a barge moored five miles above the Devil's Channel, at Island Thirty-five, along with a friend named John Bridge and a Creole crew of five. The vessel on which they traveled had set out from St. Louis with thirty thousand pounds of lead destined for sale in New Orleans, and Bradbury, an adventurous man as well as a scientist, had found the voyage so far immensely interesting. Rocks and plants he had never before seen excited his botanical and mineralogical curiosity; the sight of the many varieties of boats on the river, with their emigrants setting out for the West, stirred his imagination. Just below the Chickasaw Bluffs, they had had a tense encounter with hostile Indians who accused the travelers of shooting their dog, providing just the kind of story that would hold his English friends entranced, and the skills required of the pilot on this extraordinary river aroused his admiration. The inventiveness of Americans interested him too; he understood a steamboat had been built at Pittsburgh.

The barge reached Island Thirty-five late in the afternoon, and even the experienced pilot of the vessel would not attempt passage in darkness through the Devil's Channel, whence the roar made by the river's current rushing through the wall of trees could be heard for miles. Bradbury did wonder why the captain ordered the boat moored on a slope, but his question was answered by a shrug. On this strange, mighty river, key to the riches of a continent, almost beyond the imaginings of Western Europeans with their beautiful and more manageable rivers, only those experienced in its moods and its tortuous meanderings were privy to the secrets of navigating it successfully. If the *patron* preferred to moor the barge on a slope, no one would argue.

It was the slope that saved them. When the screaming of the wild fowl began and the violent lurching, when the cracking of trees and the rumbling under the earth and the roar of the foaming river brought them awake, they felt the dreadful lift of the river's swell as the perpendicular banks upstream and below crashed down, but their vessel rode the rise. From the terrified crew came the cry, "O mon Dieu! Nous perirons!" and by the light of the fire kept burning at the stern they saw the roll of the waters and the rise and fall of trees on its surface bobbing like toys, saw all around them the earth's agonized upheaval and heard the fearful sounds of its torment, smelled the sulphur in the air. Like Pierce and his company, they waited the night; like them, they survived.

There were others whose stories we know. There was Captain John Davis, in a company of forty boats moored at the twenty-fifth island, awakened by "the greatest emotion that can possibly be supposed of the boat, which compared to a team of horses running away with a wagon over the most rocky road in the country." Cast off by the river's swell into the current beside the island, he and the others anchored their vessels there until dawn, counting fifty shocks before daylight came and with it that terrible seven o'clock in the morning quake that no one who had felt it would ever forget. They lost three boats in their passage down the river. One man was rescued from the branches of the snag against which his boat was wrecked, rescued after he had hung there for four hours, while the branch to which he clung sank deeper and deeper until the waters were inches away, when a skiff passed close by, close enough. He fell into it.

There was Captain Sarpy of St. Louis, with his family, who anchored on the evening of December fifteenth at Island Ninety-four, in the middle of Nine-Mile Reach, not far from Vicksburg, where the view of the river was especially beautiful and the landing good. It did not strike him as strange that only his vessel took shelter there; after all, other islands lay close, above and below, and as dusk fell, the family moved contentedly about the boat. A flatboat passed and those aboard waved, called out something. The Sarpys waved back. The friendly callers waved again with surprising heartiness, almost frenzy, as the current carried them away. Soon, on this overcast night, all vessels afloat save local ones familiar with each bend and turn and snag would tie up until day, but even as the light waned, a skiff appeared from the settlement on the opposite shore, being rowed hard against the stream toward Island Ninety-four. Curious—

They did not come ashore, just called, working their oars. Captain Sarpy? Captain Sarpy! Word had been passed of his coming, and of the money he carried. Didn't he know that Island Ninety-four was Stack Island, the Crow's Nest? Was he insane? Stack Island! Haunt of pirate gangs for years past, frequented until his death a few years earlier by Samuel Mason, one-time Revolutionary hero who formed one of the region's most powerful pirate gangs. The island had a splendid view of the river for seeing potential victims approach; experienced rivermen passed it with rifles ready and watchful eyes.

Nervously, the Sarpy family lifted lines and dropped quietly downriver to Island Ninety-five, where other boats were moored and crews were armed. They relaxed.

Until the river convulsed and the crockery fell and the children cried and the crewmen leaped on to the deck, scrambling for safety in the dark. Here the shocks were weaker, the devastation less than higher upriver, but the continual roaring and the trembling of the earth and the frenzied motion of the vessel held them in terror until morning, when they saw on the river and on the shore the marks of the terrible visitation. They saw out on the river the floating trees and the matted rafts of debris, saw the swirling foam and the continuous heaving of the agitated stream, looked in awe at one another and then, at someone's cry of astonishment, looked upstream. There was no Island Ninety-four. Where it had been were only swirling water and a mass of wreckage. No living being moved.

Not only islands vanished. What of a lake? A lake three hundred yards long and one hundred wide, of clear water and well stocked with fish, escaping in the night by two parallel fissures about eight yards apart. It had been Mr. Hunter's and was not far from Little Prairie and was called Lake Eulalie. What of Mr. Culberson's smokehouse and well, moved during the night to the other side of the Mississippi? A mountain was ripped apart at Knoxville, Tennessee, with a terrible noise and flashes of fire, and water issued from the fissure created, water hot to the touch—a sign! Camp meetings in the region, not so well attended earlier, drew enormous, hysterical crowds. In Asheville, North Carolina, rocks moved and hills were shaken. In Charleston, South Carolina, church bells rang seemingly of their own accord, and in New York City clocks stopped and buildings trembled.

The Indians did not write of their experience; they did not have to. Those empty canoes so sadly visible, like the abandoned family boats, were silent witnesses to terror and loss. The gaping chasms in Indian country, the broken trees, the bodies of deer and bear and other familiar creatures told not only of devastation but of shock to an ancient way of life. Where the fissures were formed, new creeks were made, Seneca Creek and Honey Cypress and Buffalo Creek, Raglin and Taylor Sloughs, all of them running northwesterly and southeasterly as the fissures had. But the most enduring, the most dramatic testimony, was, is, Reelfoot Lake. In what was Chickasaw country in Tennessee, where before that terrible night Indian towns and rich hunting grounds had been, a lake was made fifty miles long and three to twenty wide, parts of it shallow, parts fifty to one hundred feet deep. Within it, oak and walnut and cypress stand branchless beneath the water that is clear as mountain water, with nothing of the river's mud. And fish swim in and out among the trees.

Scientists lost no time in speculating on the causes of the quake, nor did others less informed. Puzzled by the occurrence of an earthquake in a region so far from volcanic regions or the sea, those versed in geology talked of subsidence or of artesian pressures from below; learned papers were written and discussed. But others had their own ideas. On his way downriver, with the shocks continuing, John Bradbury spoke to a resident of the Lower Chickasaw Bluffs, who told him whence the trouble came. The earth, he said, had rolled over one of the two horns of the comet and was lodged between them. It was trying desperately to surmount the other horn, and until it did there would be no peace. If it failed, ah, then! the world would surely be destroyed. A writer in the *Louisiana Gazette,* however, knew the folly of such wild fancies; he had followed the news and had a more reasonable hypothesis. The comet, he suggested, having passed its perihelion and moved westward, had perhaps touched the mountains of California and "given a small shake to this side of the globe."

On the night of December fifteenth, Jared Brooks was thinking without urgency of what stories would be run in the next issue of the *Louisville Gazette,* due to appear five days hence. There would be "Ship News" of course; there always was. There would be the latest dispatches from the East concerning British arrogance and the possibility of war; the *Richmond Enquirer* was regularly publishing a blacklist of vessels illegally boarded. Dispatches had come also from Europe: Napoleon, with practically all of Europe in hand, was engaged with the British fleet; there was a report that he considered the comet an auspicious sign for an invasion of Russia. Hostilities in West Florida were continuing.

Brooks need not have thought at all; his story was thrust upon him. As chimneys fell and the earth trembled, as windows rattled and Louisville commerce lurched to a halt—what vessel dared leave?—as he counted the shocks (in thirteen weeks he would count 1,874) he forgot the dispatches. And after the first alarm had subsided and it appeared that Louisville would suffer only mild damage, he thought of the steamboat. How had it fared? Word came in slowly of the devastation below (the full story was never told, so poor was communication), of the earth's fury and the rivers' turbulence and of vessels lost; and as it did, there was a sad agreement among their friends—even some who had not wished the vessel well felt sadness—that Lydia and Nicholas Roosevelt, with their two small children, might never be seen again.

8

It was 2:00 A.M., that morning of December 16. Lydia woke suddenly, as one awakes to a noise, a feeling, an awareness of *something*. The children were sleeping; it could not have been Henry's first tentative whimper of hunger, a sound that could bring her awake in an instant, nor was Rosetta tossing, as she sometimes did with a bad dream. Then she saw in the candlelight that Nicholas was already awake, moving toward the door of the cabin.

"What is it?" she called softly.

"I don't know. Feels like we're grounded," he said, just as softly, and was gone.

How could they ground? Unless the cables were cut! Indians? Indians were always the first thought, pirates next. But the water could have fallen during the night, or the current changed. Even as the possibilities flickered through her mind, she knew their remoteness. The crew was too careful, Jack and Baker too skilled.

Fully awake now, alarmed, Lydia pulled on her robe, put her feet on the floor—and felt it shudder, felt herself thrown suddenly off balance, her stomach quiver with nausea.

Dear God, what could it be? She moved quickly toward the   *129* children, both of them awake now, Henry crying, Rosetta sitting up wide-eyed and shivering. Lydia realized that the weather had turned suddenly cold. The cabin shook and trembled, stopped, trembled again.

The maid appeared, her hair awry—but still pretty, Lydia thought irrelevantly; Baker should see her now.

"Oh, ma'am, what is it? Is it Indians?" She was shaking.

"No! No. Of course not. Just—let's get the children dressed." But even as she spoke bravely, her own heart was pounding. She listened tensely for sounds from the deck, trying to discern what was happening above. There were footsteps and voices, and then Nicholas was with them, his face grave. "It's an earthquake, Lyddy. Get dressed and come out on deck. It's better there."

An earthquake? Impossible. Earthquakes happened in places you read about, in Pompeii, in Lisbon, in New Spain, not on solid North American ground! Quickly she dressed and helped bundle up the children—the nurse had appeared, shaken too—and they hurried out on deck. But there it was no better. With Rosetta nestling beside her and the baby in her arms and Tiger moaning strangely as he prowled the deck or came to put his head against her, she could still feel the trembling of the vessel as the shocks traveled along the cable from the bank. Ashore, the trees made a sobbing sound while the river lurched and rolled, and the cries of night birds mingled with the frightened, questioning calls of swans and wild geese roused into blind, panicky flight. In the heavy darkness, it was almost impossible to distinguish shapes, but as one looked, there became visible a continuing disturbance among the trees, as if from a wind—but there was no wind. For long moments the boat would be still, swaying gently, and then would come the long, sighing shudder and the trembling of the deck and a distant rumbling sound like thunder, and all aboard would stop talking and wait, wait until steadiness returned. The shrill tone of voices as talking resumed told of the tension that held them all. Conversation began, then dwindled off; one of the crew, walking away, muttered something that no one understood, something about a judgment, and the group stirred uneasily, with a ripple of nervous laughter.

Nicholas had been pacing the deck, talking with Andrew Jack, and now he stopped before them. They would leave at first dawn, he said, as soon as there was light enough to distinguish shapes in the water; if the quake continued, as was unlikely, they would all be safer on the river than ashore, and chances were they would soon pass out of the perimeters of the disturbance. Oh, there've been earth tremors here before! he remarked with great casualness, but they were nothing to worry about. Certainly not on the water.

No one thought of going back to sleep, save the children. The hands were gathered on deck, waiting for orders. Jack and Baker moved about, the light from their lanterns throwing wavering, grotesque shadows against the machinery amidships. Lydia, uneasy despite Nicholas's reassurances, marveled at the loyalty and courage of this crew that so far had not complained or shown reluctance to continue on this voyage that seemed to have some hostile force setting up hindrances in its way. Even the weather had declared itself their enemy, so unseasonably hot and oppressive had it been and then so darkly, dismally cold.

Daylight brought little change in the brooding atmosphere. The shocks continued, the sun was barely visible, there was a faint, unpleasant smell of sulphur in the air, and a spitting, spiteful rain had begun to fall. But as the vessel got under way, as the jarring of the engine and the monotonous beating of the wheels set up a vibration that covered any other, as breakfast was served in the forward cabin to the Roosevelts and then to the maids and the officers (always a merry gathering that) and then to the crew as was customary, everyone's spirits lifted. In years to come, visitors from other lands, especially if they traveled on steamboats, would be appalled at the grim ferocity with which Americans attacked their food, at the lack of courtesy or conversation at meals, but here on the *New Orleans* there was an intimacy, even between master and crew, that made for easy communication and banter. As Nicholas took time to talk with one group and then another, promising that they would soon be passing out of the center of the disturbance and would make better time than ever with the coal aboard and that they would stop overnight at Henderson to show off the steamboat to old friends 131 and possible subscribers and give the crew a night ashore, the earlier enthusiasm was revived; there were smiles again.

It was later in the day, as they approached Henderson, that first one and then another aboard found himself glancing toward the others in fearful questioning. For now even the noise of the engine and the beating of the wheels, even a determination not to hear what was there to be heard, could not hide the grinding, rushing sound of ripping earth, of violent splashing as great pieces of bank tore away and fell into the river, carrying with them the bordering trees. Not far from the mouth of the Green River, they passed a cluster of people gathered about a flatboat pulled up on shore, partly crushed. A man lay on the ground, and a group of women, clothes sodden and clinging, were retrieving what they could from the vessel while they motioned to the children to stay away from the banks. Every few minutes, when the earth trembled, they would all stop at once and become a tableau of terror as they paused in their frantic salvaging to stare at one another and then at the river, at the sky, the trees, as if searching, searching. Where can we go? Where is it safe? Where? Where? Lydia herself felt a sudden fear and again the terrible doubts. Should she have brought her children on this voyage? Had she a right? She consoled herself by remembering Nicholas's sensible observation that they might very well be avoiding the full force of the earthquake by proceeding downriver. How did they know that Louisville itself was not the focus of the disturbance? Besides, what was so unusual about a tree fallen into the river? It happened all the time as pieces of the bank were washed away. Perhaps what they were seeing gave an exaggerated idea of the quake's severity and range.

In any case, they could not go back. Not now. Not only would any attempt to turn back so late in the season mean braving the imminent approach of ice, it would be impossible to take the *New Orleans* past the Falls and unthinkable to leave her. And what an ignominious defeat it would be to give up now after all the worry, the struggle, and the triumph at the Falls! No, they would go on. They must.

If only she could quell this gnawing, fluttering feeling of panic.

As they drew near Henderson, visible from several miles away—for the river held no bend here to hide it from view—Lydia, along with all those aboard, felt at least tentatively a sense of relief. Throngs were gathering on the bluff just as one would expect; a few figures could be seen straggling down to the landing and a few, more distant, running toward the woods behind the town. (The frightened ones; there were always a few.) From a distance, at least, it looked wonderfully ordinary, undisturbed. The quake might not have reached here at all. If it had not, there would probably be a horse race along Elm Street to welcome them; George Holloway would be offering supplies from his general store; Dr. Rankin and his wife would no doubt be delighted to bring their thirteen children aboard to see the steamboat up close; Mr. Patterson, whose plantation they had passed five miles upstream, would likely have set off on horseback to be there to greet them. As Jack turned the wheel to round to and Baker ordered the fire lowered, the steam went roaring up to announce their coming and everyone aboard looked anxiously toward shore, hopeful of release from the uncertainty and fear the day had brought.

They drew close, heading for the landing. The figures on shore became distinct, the buildings and houses separate and identifiable, and someone exclaimed: "The chimneys! Look at the chimneys!" They looked, and groaned. Chimneys were down, fallen, toppled. Rubble lay in the streets of Henderson; the crowd had gathered not in excited welcome but in shared misery. Any wonder at the steamboat's arrival was dimmed in the greater emotion of fear, and in the anxious hope that those aboard the *New Orleans* might know what had happened elsewhere, happened to others—family, friends. Later, when Nicholas and Lydia had come ashore and seen the damage and reported what they knew, some of their friends told them—in a desperate attempt at humor—that they would be held responsible for the loss of their servants. The sight of the smoking steamboat on top of the quake had been too much for them, and they had fled into the woods, perhaps never to return!

But that was the only humor to be found that day or night, as the shocks continued and the people of Henderson had more 133 immediate concerns than the presence of even so remarkable a vessel. When the *New Orleans* left next morning, Nicholas was feeling aggrieved. How could one compete with an earthquake? Lydia, knowing how much the skepticism of certain friends had hurt him and wanting his vindication as much as he did, had almost to agree—it didn't seem fair. She wished she could believe, as he really seemed to, that they would soon be out of the quake area, but she could not. Even when he gathered the company on deck and brusquely gave his assessment of their situation, that the shocks had already continued longer than had ever been known in the region, or anywhere else, as far as he knew, and therefore must reasonably be expected to come to an end soon, and that the safest place to be, in any event, was on the water, she felt no reassurance. Neither, it seemed, did anyone else. The doubt evident in their expressions, their lack of response, spoke clearly, and on her husband's face Lydia saw for just an instant—in a twitch of the cheek, a tightened jaw—that he, too, felt more concern than he was willing to profess. Nevertheless, he spoke challengingly: Well, wasn't it so? No one answered.

Oh, please! Lydia prayed. Don't let them fail him now! Her eyes caught Andrew Jack's, pleaded. He hesitated, smiled faintly, and then stepped forward.

"Aye, aye, sir," he said, in a voice almost hearty, and looked around at the others. There was a general murmur, a shuffling of feet, then "Aye, aye, sir's" in low tones. They went slowly to their stations.

Whatever the misgivings, they were for the most part concealed as the *New Orleans* made her way past and around the islands that lay beyond Henderson. At Highland Creek, few of the villagers at the little settlement were visible. Here, too, the chimneys showed damage, and, along the shore, gaps in the cane brakes appeared where great clumps of earth had fallen into the river, shaken away by the shocks. Lydia found that she could predict each shock as she sat on deck, for just before it began, Tiger would come to her, moaning softly, and put his head in her lap. She tried to read and found it impossible, tried to sew and gave up, finally went to stand beside Nicholas as, silent now, he stopped now here, now there to inspect a rope, a stanchion. His orders to the crew were minimal, their responses barely audible, but if he felt any irritation, as he might have under other circumstances, he showed none now.

They reached the wide, beautiful Wabash and the end of Indiana Territory. Now the Territory of the Illinois lay to their right, with Shawnee Town directly ahead; beyond stretched some fifty miles of wilderness, with no settlement worth noting. At this point, the region below the Ohio was claimed by the various Indian tribes as a common hunting ground. For years, Choctaws and Cherokees and Chickasaws and the tribes above the Ohio had fought over it until at last a truce was made, and by agreement all three tribes shared the land. When Virginians intruded some years earlier, resentment, especially among the Chickasaws, was keen, and travelers along the river had learned to be especially alert here to Indian mischief.

Usually this part of the river, near Shawnee Town, was merry with the singing and the obvious pleasure of keelers and bargers as they approached the town where a night of carousing was thought their due, but now the crews of the few vessels moving downriver—none were coming up—were silent, clearly frightened. Some did stand atop the cabins the better to see the steamboat as it passed, and waved desultorily, but there were no shouts and questions, none of the usual banter of river encounters. And any hope that at Shawnee Town there would be reason for cheer was shattered as the steamboat drew near and those aboard saw here, too, among the thirty or so cabins and houses and taverns and dram shops, downed chimneys and broken fences and a terrified populace huddling in little clusters away from buildings that shook even as the *New Orleans* passed. At the landing place a great tree lay crosswise against the bank.

That night they rounded to at Island Eighty-seven, opposite the notorious Cave in Rock, that splendid cavern a hundred and twenty feet deep, with its great cathedral arch and its thousands of names scratched on the limestone walls, haunt for years of river pirates only recently driven out. On the flatboat trip, the stop

Snags in the river. From a mid-nineteenth-century illustration in *Harper's New Monthly Magazine*.

here had been one of delight for Nicholas and Lydia. They had visited the cave itself, wondered at the perfect arch of its opening, and inspected the carvings in the rock, but the stop this night brought only greater fear. With the mooring of the vessel and the quieting of the engine and wheels, the shuddering of the cables and occasional lurching of the boat became all too evident. As the night wore on, the agitation of the shore, where the trees writhed and trembled, seemed to increase, and those aboard lay tense, trying in vain to sleep.

They found next morning that the water had risen during the night; a sandbar downstream, usually visible even at high water, was covered, as were some of the landmarks along the shore. The *New Orleans* had been moored far out in the water on a long cable for fear of falling trees; now she appeared to be even farther out in the stream, for the river waters reached past the bank into the woods and lay restless and muddy among the trees. The crew showed in haggard faces and quick tempers the effects of the sleepless night, and when the man who had earlier muttered about a judgment began proclaiming in sepulchral tones, "There will be pestilences and famines and earthquakes in various places . . . ," one or two shouted "Shut up!" and there was a general growl of anger.

After they had loosed the cables and gone downstream some distance, it was evident that the steamboat was working harder than before but not traveling any faster; Nicholas, going into the engine room to consult with Baker, found him speaking with unusual roughness to his men. He looked worried. Yes, he said, the furnace was using more fuel to make the same speed as before. The current had slowed, a sure sign that the Mississippi was in flood. And didn't Mr. Roosevelt see how muddy the water was?

From Andrew Jack, Nicholas found no cheer. The pilot was frowning as he studied the waters that spread beyond the banks, watching for a channel that had suddenly become elusive, trying to avoid the many snags that had been made of trees cast into the stream. He swore when he found that the tips of islands had broken off to slip into the stream and leave bluff edges that destroyed the gradual approach that made rounding them easy. The charts so carefully prepared, as well as Zadoc Cramer's directions, were almost useless; now progress depended on his mastery of navigation and the sixth sense on which a pilot depended on an unknown stream. Around each bend lay another wide expanse of overflow that turned the forests into swamp. Where there were no bluffs, it was hard to distinguish where river ended and shore began.

As they moved carefully along what seemed to be the channel, noting that the signs of damage seemed to be increasing rather than diminishing and that the shocks were continuing, they became more and more aware of a presence they had been trying to ignore. Settlements were few here on the Kentucky side of the river, fewer still on the Illinois, and below lay the Indian hunting grounds. Now among the boles of the trees, which stood knee deep in water, canoes passed in and out. Some were paddled swiftly away as the steamboat approached; others, though, as if on a dare or simply to show some newfound courage, were brought closer than any had come before. Had the Indians lost the superstitious dread that had made them keep their distance? *137*

Or had the terror of the earthquake convinced them that *Penelore,* the Fire Canoe, must be destroyed? Had there been wild dances the night before as the earth trembled, and chants to give them courage, and exhortations from the shaman as he raised his arms to the heavens and called on their guardian spirits for help? Already the Indians associated the steamboat with the comet, linking the sparks from her chimney to the comet's fiery train. Did they now, like the squatters, hold her responsible for the earthquake too?

Lydia watched apprehensively, in growing fear, and Nicholas, knowing her feelings and remembering the fright given them when the two Indians invaded the flatboat, put his arm around her while he watched the darting vessels with a wary eye. Baker, also aware of them, put on more steam in response to Jack's commands; both knew they were taking a calculated risk. A canoe approached, then fled as a sudden spurt of steam emerged with a roar and the smoke poured from the stacks. Another came, fled. But then a group of three emerged from the woods a little ahead of the boat and came almost across her path. Rosetta, who had come out on deck with the nurse, pointed at the canoes, asking questions, the eternal What's that? What's that? Lydia, trying to be casual so as not to transmit her own fear to the child, told her they were Indians, like the Indians she'd seen in Pittsburgh—did she remember? with the feathers? They were people who liked to dance and hunt and who lived in the forest. But finally she gave up the effort to be brave, held her child close, and just watched. They came out in groups now, then retreated. Suddenly she heard one of the crew muttering to another, saw Jack turn sharply aside, and saw a great canoe, fully manned, its crew outnumbering the crew of the *New Orleans,* enter the river a little ahead and paddle swiftly toward them.

Nicholas passed the order to Baker—more steam! Jack, nervous now because of the unpredictability of the channel and a bend ahead, shouted out a protest. The steamboat could outrun the canoe, no question about it, given a clear path. But how could she maneuver at any reasonable speed along this changing stream? The high water might eliminate one danger—most of

138

the sandbars along the way were under water, but high speed downstream increased the danger of running headlong into a planter or sawyer or a wreck, or of being caught in the sudden rush of water beneath a bend.

The braves in the canoe were synchronizing their paddling like a splendid machine, the boat moving with incredible speed through the water, aided by the current. They moved ever closer as they paddled, taking advantage of the river's flow; unlike the steamboat, canoes were maneuverable whether in the channel or not. Clearly, something had taken away their fear of the Fire Canoe or given them the suicidal courage to challenge her, if indeed such was their intent. Their purposeful movements suggested that it was; they made no peaceful sign or gesture. That they would have rifles was almost sure. If they did not acquire them by stealing or in trade with unscrupulous whites, they were kept well supplied by the British—or so all Westerners were convinced.

"Get into the cabin, Lyddy!" Nicholas became suddenly aware of her standing there with Rosetta. If there was to be trouble, let the two of them, along with Henry, be protected by walls at least! Lydia obeyed, hating it. She had stood beside her husband in every danger, faced down his detractors, been totally, irrevocably loyal. And now to skulk in her cabin like some soft, frivolous woman? But for the children's sake she had no choice. As they hurried below, she told the maid to keep Rosetta quiet and content with a story, then rushed at once to the cabin window from which she could see the big canoe.

Surely the Indians must fall back! They could not possibly keep up with the power of steam. And yet at any moment the river could show its trickery (did it favor the Indians, then?), could hurl the *New Orleans* against some impassable barrier, ground her, high water or not. They were in a long reach now, with no bends to make the river ahead invisible, and Lydia could feel the increased vibration as Baker ordered wood crammed into the furnace door and the steam shut off to build up power. She knew that in the engine room the fire was leaping up, that above them the smoke stack was pouring forth smoke and burning   *139* chips and that the steam was hissing as it pushed against the weight of the safety valves. The canoe seemed to be staying even with the steamboat, so much so that neither it nor the *New Orleans* appeared to be moving if one did not look at the shore. There was one especially frightening possibility: If the Indians could move close enough to toss something into the paddle wheels, they could bring the steamboat to a grinding, terrible stop, render her helpless so that they could be joined by those others who glided in and out among the trees, watching the deadly race.

Lydia, watching, saw the canoe moving smoothly, ominously, over the wide waters, skimming the current. Her eyes followed. And then suddenly she realized that she was turning her head—turning her head! The canoe was dropping back. While the paddlers worked furiously to keep up their pace, to increase it, the *New Orleans* surged suddenly ahead with a great burst of power, one of the great paddle wheels went humping over a log with a horrible clatter, and the Indians, with wild shouts and angry gestures, gave up and retreated toward the forest from which they had come. *Penelore's* magic had won. From the crew out on deck came a shout of triumph. They'd showed them stinkin' savages!

Sobbing with relief, Lydia swooped Rosetta into her arms and moved over to Henry just as Nicholas was entering the cabin, concerned but jubilant. The steamboat had shown what she could do, hadn't she? Hadn't the engine performed wonderfully? How he wished there'd been more people to see the race! He gathered the three of them into a huge embrace and kissed away Lydia's tears. Why had she been so worried?

Laughing now, Lydia shook her head in helpless resignation. Nicholas would never admit that he was in trouble, that the problem would not go away or the challenge not be met successfully, even when he himself was the problem or the challenge. But Lydia knew that he had been as frightened as she; he was under no illusion about what could come of an Indian attack if one actually came. There would be other Indians along the way, but word might now be passed that the magic of the steamboat was more powerful than the magic of the shaman. And yes, it *was* possible, he agreed somewhat reluctantly in answer to her questioning suggestion, that the challengers were just testing their speed against that of the Fire Canoe.

Discussion of the race went on far into the evening, diverting attention to some extent from the continuing shocks and the evidence of greater damage along the shores and from the absence of any vessels coming from downriver. They lay that night at the mouth of Cash Creek, six miles above the junction with the great river that they had come to feel was expecting them. The meeting would be far different this time than it had been on the flatboat journey. Then, the limpid waters of the Ohio had carried their vessel halfway across the milky Mississippi in its eager plunge to join the stream. At that memorable moment even Nicholas, busy as he was in watching for navigational hazards and measuring the currents and checking his findings against Cramer's, had paused to look all around the wide waters and then down that majestic, turbulent way to the southern lands, to the Gulf of Mexico, to the sea, to the world—and had shaken his head in wonder. What a river! What a splendid, terrible river!

This time the sky and the earth and the water all seemed their enemy. Instead of a limpid stream to carry them into a welcome rendezvous, a great, turbid, muddy lake that churned in swirls and boils seemed trying to push them back. The point of land between the creek and the rivers' joining, covered with walnut and ash and pecan and closely tangled cane, was all awash. The settlement of Trinity was a scene of disorder, the people fearful, some of their cabins tumbled like children's playhouses by the jarring of the earth. Fort Massac, just above, was battered, too, its wooden palisades down, its buildings damaged, and in the pale light of this dreary dusk even the eagles that roosted in the bare, white-barked sycamores or glided overhead looked more ominous than beautiful against the sombre sky.

No one pretended anymore that there was no fear aboard. The crew, ebullient with victory, had joked about the Indians' challenge, but as the *New Orleans* rounded to and the fire died away, as the line was cast out and the ominous rumbling beneath the earth became audible once again, the joking stopped. Voices were lower, faces grim again. Looking at that vast expanse of swirling water and the fallen banks, everyone knew that before them lay a greater challenge than a party of Indian braves. The wicked river awaited them now, waited with a mighty current and treacherous bends, with shifting reefs and eddies and boils and tumbling snags, and with an earthquake for good measure.

There would be Indians about. Nicholas ordered a watch posted, with rifle.

9

Had they been asleep two minutes? Two hours? They had slept fitfully, a sleep of nervous exhaustion, their senses alert to sound and movements. Henry awakened soon after they came into the cabin for the night; Lydia nursed him and then had to soothe a crying Rosetta, who awakened sweaty and chilled from a bad dream. When Lydia finally fell asleep—Nicholas was already snoring—she felt that nothing less than a band of screaming Indians could wake her.

She awoke. Eyes wide open. Heart thumping. From the deck came the sound of the trampling of many feet, the shouts of the men. The cabin, with only the light from a flickering candle, was almost dark, and through the windows came no light at all. There was a cry in the forward cabin.

Nicholas was already out of the berth, springing to the only weapon at hand, the sword that hung with his ceremonial clothes brought along for official receptions. Lydia reached hurriedly for a flint, then stopped as he ordered her in a smothered voice not to strike a light.

"Stay here, Lyddy. Get the children up."

She shared his thought—Indians! Indians gliding silently in   *143* under cover of the darkness, invisible to the watch. Agile red bodies climbing stealthily aboard, determined to destroy this thing of evil whose power could move the earth. She could hardly make out Nicholas's figure as he flung open the door, sword in hand, but could not help thinking even in her panic how brave he was, how quick. But of what use was a sword? There had been no sound of gunfire from the crew. Surely they had not been so easily overpowered! Hurriedly, foolishly silent, for now both children were crying, she moved toward the door. Saw flames. . . .

Fire in the forward cabin! Not Indians, but an enemy as deadly, an enemy that all steamboats to come after would fear with a deathly fear, a destroyer that would carry out the river's vengeance on its conquerors, would scald hideously thousands of victims with that enemy's own steam, toss screaming passengers and flaming parts of vessels into the waiting river, exact a toll beyond counting as the price of victory. Along the deck of the cabin a tiny stream of fire wandered. Flames leaped from the wood by the stove, licked at the walls, the furnishings, while frantic crewmen passed back and forth, back and forth, filling the buckets, emptying them, filling them again, throwing on the flames the river water that was now their hope of salvation. They appeared and disappeared in the smoke, cursing as it curled around them and into their eyes while they tried by the unsteady light of basket torches to see what they were doing. Nicholas, sword quickly discarded, had taken command at once, was hoarsely calling out orders. Throw wet canvas over the deck! Pull down the curtains! Buckets here! Coughing from the smoke, he kicked and pushed out of the way some of the furniture about to be caught by the hungry flames, beat out dancing sparks with his hand, snatched angrily at a water bucket being passed too slowly. He saw the watch come to join in and ordered him back on guard. Who knew yet if the fire had been set?

Holding Rosetta back and motioning to the maid to pick up Henry, Lydia thought frantically of how to get the children to safety. The narrow passageway between the cabins was thronged with the crew passing back and forth. To take the children out on deck might be more dangerous than to keep them here, and the chances of getting ashore in the confusion and darkness were small. Besides, the earth was no longer solid; to take refuge where the trees themselves were shaking, the land atremble, was not to take refuge at all.

Slowly the flames subsided; water poured down the bulkheads, from the stove, the furniture, slopped over the deck. The woodwork of the cabin, one of Nicholas's great prides, was absolutely ruined. There would be no way now to make repairs, no one qualified to do so, nor any supplies for the making of them before the vessel's arrival in Natchez or even New Orleans, where she was scheduled to make her glorious entrance. The carefully joined interior work over which the craftsmen had labored so lovingly under his watchful eyes (and Lydia's too) was charred and broken, and Lydia, seeing his look of anger as he viewed the damage, knew that were they not out here, helpless to recruit others, whoever was responsible would be discharged—given Nicholas's mood, even booted—from service. He was asking questions now, while the men, dirty and wet and tousled, some of them nursing burns on forearms and hands, eyes still watering, looked from one to another and then toward the servant whose carelessness, they knew, could have cost them all their lives.

He had been assigned to the forward cabin to keep the fire going and had placed wood close to the stove in anticipation of the next day's needs. Lying down beside it himself, exhausted as was everyone else aboard after the tension of the day, he had fallen asleep. The stove became overheated, the wood took fire; still he slept on. A flame reached out, began exploring delicately the joiner's work close by, began climbing; it was joined by another, and another. . . . Happily for the sweetly dreaming crewman, they began radiating more heat than smoke, for he awoke, half suffocated, saw with horror the surrounding flames, already beyond the control of the one fire bucket ready by the stove, and choking, terrified, staggered out on deck to cry out the alarm, an alarm that brought the shouts, the trampling of feet.

But he *had* awakened in time. And how could anyone be held responsible for anything on this seemingly cursed boat? *145*

When the harsh reprimand was given, the man merely looked sullen—he hadn't signed up for an earthquake, either. In this sentiment he clearly had the sympathy of the rest of the crew, and Lydia, knowing how damaging to all of them hard feelings could be, tried to calm Nicholas down, no easy task. His temper was high and he insisted on assessing the damage at once, estimating what repairs could be made, and giving orders for the morning. Only then did he consent to return to the cabin. There, Lydia tried to find some cheer in this latest disaster. She told Nicholas how splendidly he had performed—and all the men, too! They had shown how well they could act in an emergency, hadn't they? And wasn't it lucky the fire hadn't spread farther? The men were exhausted—you could understand that. After a while, as she knew they would, his spirits lifted and he agreed. Yes, it could have been worse; at least they could still go on. He laughed at her praise of his bravery—after all, she said, it *could* have been Indians!—but she knew he was pleased. She didn't tell him that she wished her father could have seen him, seen how courageous he was, how *young*.

They were now, this third day after the shocks began, some sixty miles from New Madrid, the last town of consequence between the mouth of the Ohio and Natchez, which lay seven hundred miles down the Mississippi. They had planned to buy in New Madrid the additional supplies needed to carry them the long distance, including ready-cut wood to supplement their diminishing supply of coal, but any hope that the region farther on had been spared was fading. The encounter with the Indians, despite the steamboat's victory, threatened further trouble, and the fire had been frightening. Now evidence was mounting that more damage, not less, lay ahead. The masses of floating trees, an upturned boat or two, the continuing sultriness of the air, and the earth's recurrent rumblings made cheerful words seem hollow. All of them fell silent as they moved slowly on.

Very slowly. For where, exactly, was the channel?

From the Ohio they had entered the Mississippi in a southeasterly direction; now they were traveling southwest. With the charts almost useless and landmarks gone, Jack was following the course of the current's swiftest flow, probably the sign of the channel. The way was impeded by snags; eddies and ripples churned and swirled; and even the broad, usually calmer, reaches of the river were troubled and turbulent. On the boat the tension seemed to reach physically from one to another. Mr. Roosevelt's suggestion that once they were on the big river the force of the earthquake might be proportionately diminished had stirred faint hope, but so far there were no signs that he was right. They had gone twenty miles from the point of entry when they approached the Iron Banks, perpendicular bluffs beneath which a dangerous eddy formed. Here, some crumbling of the high banks was continuous, but now those aboard saw with dismay that far more than ordinary crumbling was taking place. Acres and acres, huge chunks, of the wide bluffs had fallen in, were still falling, the rust-colored earth sinking into muddy water that was reddish brown, as though mixed with blood. Ahead, they knew, lay Wolf Island, some forty square miles of timbered land where James Hunter, a farmer and professional gambler ("the only man I ever knew who seemed to take a pride in letting it be known," wrote Cramer), kept an extensive settlement. At its head, a sandbar cut three-quarters of the way across the river. That they expected. What they did not expect was to see the island itself partially submerged, its fifteen thousand acres almost covered with river water, trees toppled along the banks and others tangled with one another as if tied. Mr. Hunter's stock, cattle and hogs and geese, were huddled together on the prairie in the center of the island. At the foot of the bar, where landing was good, a few flatboats, apparently deserted, were moored. Just beyond, a man standing on the deck of another, close against the cabin as though ready to retreat, watched the steamboat's approach, then, evidently convinced that those aboard this floating, smoking sawmill were neither pirates nor supernatural visitors, waved frantically, waved again, raised his arms high as though in appeal.

"Can't be no pirate decoy," one of the crew ventured, familiar with the old trick. "Not on that there island." He looked inquiringly toward Roosevelt. But Nicholas gave no signal to stop. He and Jack were standing together at the wheel, Jack clearly agitated, Nicholas for once silent, frowning at the river ahead, with its crosscurrents and shifting bars, its ripples and sunken wrecks, and those snags that could pierce a hull like a lance. The water was thick with mud thrown up from the bottom, and on its red-brown surface meandering paths of foam floated like giants' spittle. Some of the upturned trees were hoary with riverbed scrapings; they bobbed mockingly in the vessel's path as though summoned from their ancient tombs simply to block the way. Where the channel passed to the right of Island Seven and the left of Eight a huge planter seemed so firmly rooted as to be growing in the water. Signaling constantly to Baker, Jack maneuvered the boat around the obstructions, the paddle wheels revolving so slowly that they themselves appeared to be probing for what lay ahead. Lydia had come out on deck with Henry in her arms and was watching, as were all those not busy in the engine room or galley, all of them leaning forward as if on signal, turning their heads as one to see a giant tree go by. Even as they watched, they saw a mighty sycamore that had surely stood a century or more topple heavily from the bank and fall sprawling, bare branches clawing at the air, into the muddy stream.

And then they reached Island Number Ten, that island remembered by anyone who had ever stopped there as a paradise of birds, alive with song—and gasped in one collective sigh.

On the island itself and on the opposite shore, the banks had fallen by several feet. Behind the banks, trees were monstrously entangled, intertwined, great branches clinging to one another in grotesque embrace, some prevented from falling by the leaning together of others and some split straight up the middle, from root to branch, forty feet and higher, ripped apart, the separate sides of the trunk straddling fissures three and four feet wide that had opened directly beneath. No one alone could believe what he saw; it had to be confirmed by agreement—"Do you see?" "Yes! It can't be!" Strange funnellike holes pocked the earth. The willow point on the near shore was fractured as if a willful child-giant had taken a hammer to it; its surface was a mass of broken trees. Among them a flock of confused-looking crows hopped aimlessly from branch to branch, sobered perhaps by the sight of the corpses of their fellows strewn over the driftwood that bumped against the shore along with those of squirrels and rabbits and opossums and, unlikely company, a small brown bear. In broken patterns above them, flocks of duck wavered, some of them lighting tentatively on the shore, then rising again, settling, rising. On bare branches a few buzzards, already replete, contemplated the richness of the feast.

Hardly anyone spoke. The river foamed, swirled; the boat careened as the starboard wheel brushed a great raft made up of matted driftwood. On the far side of it a canoe floated, empty. Three miles below the island, they passed the mouth of the bayou that curved in from above, a point from which they should be able to see New Madrid several miles ahead. Just then, though, someone exclaimed, incredulous, pointing toward the grove of cottonwood and willow just below the bayou—or what had been a grove. Its every tree was stripped of branches; the bare, stark trunks stood like thin, immobilized soldiers leaning backward against the north wind, leaning *upstream,* against the river's flow. No trees did that! It was almost as though—but surely it couldn't have happened—the river itself had reversed its flow and flung them back in one tremendous sweep. There was no reason to the scene. There were no useful words.

Nicholas had planned to put in at Chepousa Creek, just above New Madrid. Its mouth offered safe harbor, or always had, and whatever the damage in town, there should be rivermen sheltering there who would have some word of what downriver conditions were. With anxiety now—nothing was certain anymore—they all watched the steamboat's progress. Slowly they drew near to the middle of the great bend in which New Madrid stood to the right on a handsome bluff, and Baker ordered the engines readied for the landing while Jack stood by to round to. It was almost noon.

"Dear Lord!" Jack was the first to glimpse what lay ahead. And then all of them saw.

The town had stood well above the river, commanding a

view of the stream for miles above and below. Now, as though an enormous spatula had dug in and pulled some of its base from beneath it, New Madrid lay lower by fifteen feet, its houses and buildings tumbled; beyond it lay a wide lake where the plain had been. In the surrounding area chasms hundreds of feet in length and twenty or thirty feet wide had been ripped through the earth, running northeast to southwest in parallel lines; where no fissures were, the yawning mouths of circular holes pocked the earth. Bodies from the graveyard near the shore, coffins and corpses, lay thrown on the ground as if in a hideous game or bobbed about in the river's swell. Logs and clapboard that had been parts of houses, stables, fences lay about; pigs and dogs and cattle wandered seeking firm ground, stepping over the bodies of their fellows. Over all lay a sulphurous stench. And at the mouth of the Chepousa, upturned boats swayed in the water, trees and other river debris cluttered the stream, and a few figures of rivermen wandered about as though in a daze. The scene was not real. It was impossible, a dream. Could anyone here who was still alive be sane?

On the sunken shore of the river a throng of people were gathered; they had waited together in a frightened group at the steamboat's first appearance, but as she approached, as they saw people aboard, they came suddenly in a frenzied rush toward the bank, waving, calling. There was no fear of *Penelore* here! Nicholas ordered the vessel stopped; the wheels hesitated, slowed, while those aboard, stunned and unbelieving, continued to stare in horror at the scene, conscious, now that the noise of the engine had stopped, of the occasional rumbling, like distant thunder, that came from beneath the earth.

Andrew Jack waited. Baker waited. The crew waited. Lydia spoke for them all, softly, as seemed appropriate.

"What are we going to do, Mr. Roosevelt?" What are we going to do? What are *you* going to do, Nicholas, with all of us? With your children? Why are we here? Why are we here at all?

From the *New Orleans* rose wreaths of smoke as the furnace burned low. She sat as quietly as the restless river would let her. Jack looked expectantly at Nicholas, waiting for the order to round to.

A rowboat set out from the shore. A messenger? A friend? There were several people in it—no, more than several. It was crowded with what appeared to be a number of families, the babies in arms, the men throwing sacks and carpet bags into the boat so that it seemed it must surely sink under the weight. Evidently they were leaving the town, taking their chances on the river, moving on. Where could they be going, Lydia wondered. What could they know of what lay below? What hope had they? She saw them rowing frantically across the current.

"They are trying to reach us!" She turned to Nicholas in consternation. "They want to come aboard."

It was impossible! To bring them aboard would be disastrous, would destroy them all. Even if they had supplies enough for all—and now, with no more to be gotten, they had hardly enough for themselves—these frightened, panicked people would overload the vessel, make it hopeless to try to navigate in the dangerous waters. There were too many. Too many. Where would you stop? Where call a halt? You simply could not begin. And yet, as she saw the women holding their children close to them, fleeing the ruins of their homes, as she saw another boat set out, as she hugged her own child to her, Lydia knew that she could not will herself to turn them away. How could they be refused? And yet *how could they not?* Must all die when some could live? What was the answer? What had ever been the answer? She felt caught in some parable, or in a vast cosmic game in which they all were pieces, some to be sacrificed, some saved. But she was a player in the game, as was Nicholas—Oh, Nicholas, you make the move!

He was grim, watching the approaching boats. The *New Orleans* had slackened speed; Jack was prepared to round to. The boat would soon meet the rowboats, run them down unless they changed direction. The rowers seemed bewildered and yet desperate, trying to reach the steamboat and not knowing what her next move would be. On the landing, more people had gathered, awaiting the outcome, waiting to see. Other rowboats, those still whole, were being readied while men and women and children huddled in a frightened mass, looking for some way out, any way out, of their suddenly shattered world. They were, thought Lydia, like frightened sheep, suddenly aware of the narrow gate of the slaughtering pen. She could not bring herself to say anything to Nicholas, could not actually suggest that they leave them and could not suggest that they not. I am a coward, she told herself angrily. I don't want to be the cruel one, the ruthless one, even though I *know* we can't take them. I want him to have the guilt.

Silently she turned to see what he would do. Just as silently he gave the signal to Jack, and then to Baker. Go on. They would not stop at New Madrid, would not stop.

As they drew off, the wheels churning the water, smoke pouring from the stack, they almost swamped the rowboats. Lydia turned her face away.

No one spoke for a while. There was nothing to say. Lydia gave little Henry over to the nurse, told her to have Rosetta given her dinner and her nap, and went to stand beside Nicholas. For a short time he stood there, saying nothing, then, with a shrug of his big shoulders, he went briskly about the boat, giving orders here and there, shouting to Baker above the noise of the engine. Lydia, still stunned and feeling guilty, continued to watch the broken shore and the river ahead, and knew that Nicholas's careful soundings taken on the flatboat trip had been a waste of time (but not a waste, that memorable trip!). Chutes that had shot through narrow necks projecting from the shore had been overwhelmed by the surging current and become cutoffs. Through them now the river itself flowed, making islands of what had been points of land. Huge rafts of logs floated on the foamy surface of the water; new eddies had formed under broken bluffs; sandbars had emerged where deep water had been. It was a new river and not new; on the Mississippi, only no change at all would be a novelty. They passed a flatboat whose occupants merely looked up dully at the *New Orleans,* showing little interest. It was as though in this enormous calamity, this earth change in which nobody could believe, anything less, even a vessel of fire and smoke, was of no consequence.

All day, voices were hushed. The crew talked hardly at all; their "Aye, aye, sir" emerged as though they were being respectful of the dead. And perhaps they were. The empty flatboats, the frantic, benumbed people, the devastation, the continuing agitation of the earth and the waters upon it were visible signs of unknown bodies over which the vessel had surely passed, of the anguish and fear of those lost, of travelers whose voyage had been to death. And in late evening, when they passed Little Prairie and saw the forest, tangled and torn, that adjoined the town, its gnarled and twisted limbs extended in agonized supplication, the stripped branches gaunt—what of them were left—saw Little Prairie itself sunk and destroyed and all its inhabitants evidently gone save for two or three figures wandering over the desolate land, they felt they were viewing a vision of apocalypse. Most unnatural was the purposeless flight of the birds, wheeling suddenly into the air, fluttering, dropping, calling continuous raucous cries. Ducks and geese, great trumpeter swans caught in their migration, passenger pigeons disoriented, torn from their huge flocks, even the soaring eagles, seemed confused and lost. Only the vultures sitting like hooded death on the bare branches of stripped trees or hopping toward some bloated thing were as they always were. On the muddy water floated barrels of flour, of pork, of whisky, drifted empty canoes, family boats. Whose were they? Who lay below?

The night, spent at the foot of one of the many islands below Little Prairie, was again one of sleeplessness, of the chill of terror with every shudder of the earth, every untoward noise. When they set off at dawn—and everyone saw in everyone else his own haggardness and fear—they expected nothing else but what they saw, the familiar broken shore, the drifting debris of lost voyages, the appalling river forests made up of disgorged and fallen trees. At Island Twenty-five, above Long Reach, they saw that acres of land had fallen in. At Long Reach itself the river was an impassable mass of roots and trees among which the wreckage of three boats (they would learn later that they were those lost by the Davis party) lay visible. The great raft of trees almost spanned the river and completely blocked the channel.

Four of the crew, armed with axes and poles, launched the rowboat. They went willingly; action was better than the monotony of fear. Sounding all the time, they pushed and hacked, *153* and pushed and hacked, two of them at the oars to fight the current that seemed determined to drive the small boat into the great tangled mass or to flip it around and smash it as it had not yet been able to smash the presumptuous vessel that had spawned it. Hack and push with the poles, hack. . . .

In the quiet of the waiting, with the engine stilled and the paddle wheels at rest, the intermittent sound of subterranean thunder was audible. When it came, the workers on the raft paused and waited; ashore a piece of the bank might fall or there would be the crash of timbers. Once, most horrifyingly, there came a sudden boiling of the water near the steamboat, and a noxious smell of gases filled the air as a geyser erupted from the red-brown depths, vomiting sand and sticks and mud. When at last the exhausted men had done and Baker ordered the fires high and the *New Orleans* snaked her way through the narrow gap they had made, all those aboard were holding their breath. Hardly a word was spoken save in whispers; only the voices of Rosetta and little Henry kept to their normal tones. For the feeling was over all of them that even to raise one's voice would start another shaking of the earth, would topple trees, would anger further the hostile river that had gone on this wild rampage in collusion with the powers that governed the earth. But as the day wore on, the violence seemed less. Everywhere still were the marks of upheaval, but there seemed—there *did* seem, one said and then another, carefully—to be less turbulence in the water, less agitation ashore; the vessel felt steadier.

By late afternoon they were approaching Island Thirty-two, and with the coal almost exhausted and traveling downstream in the darkness unthinkable, Nicholas gave orders to round to at the foot of the island, where the boat would be protected from the great trees being swept down by the current. There would be time for wooding up before dark, and next day, God willing and from all the signs, they might pass beyond the region of the most terrible violence. As she stood on deck with Nicholas when the boat had been tied up as far out in the river as the line would permit, Lydia felt for the first time in days a sense of tranquillity and hope. The Indians along this part of the river seemed to offer no threat; they appeared chastened and dulled by the shocks they had experienced and when they were encountered showed a measure of sad friendliness rather than hostility. All mankind was on the same side now. Perhaps, just perhaps, the terror and anxiety might really be coming to an end. That the boat had so far come through without serious damage was surely miraculous; God must be watching over them after all. The others aboard seemed to share her hopes, and Rosetta was merry again, reflecting the tentative lifting of the pall that had been hanging over all of them. Perhaps tonight they would sleep.

Few of them did. Even if their lingering fears had let them, the wild noises of the night would not. Despite the evident lessening of the earth's agitation and the river's turmoil, it seemed that more driftwood than ever came banging against the hull, sometimes with blows so sharp that the vessel trembled as she had with the earth's vibrations. Scratching sounds reminded Lydia and Nicholas of some anxious night spent between Natchez and New Orleans on their earlier voyage. At Natchez they had abandoned the damaged flatboat for a rowboat, and for four of the next nine nights on the river slept in it on buffalo robes, hearing the alligators scratch and scrabble against its wides. Then, a blow with a cane had frightened the creatures away, but no cane would be useful now. Strange gurgling sounds unlike any they had heard before made them toss and wonder, and once there was a tug on the cable that brought them both bolt upright and sent Nicholas out to investigate. He came back to report that all was quiet, as quiet as was possible on a vessel where frightened people lay awake, as quiet as could be expected where the earth was unstable, the river's current strong, the night birds flying, where the cries of owls and the howling of wolves and the calls of panthers echoed and driftwood rasped and clashed on the surface of the stream. Slowly the night wore on, muttering. The trees moaned, the river roared, every little while came a distant thunder—and then one's heart stopped.

And in the morning. . . . No wonder the night had been noisy! For the current had swept them along, hawser and all. By what miracle had they missed the hazards, escaped being grounded, not been caught in the grasping branches of the thousands of trees that the current carried past? The boat was not moving now, the hawser apparently caught on a submerged snag, and it was miracle indeed that the snag had found the hawser instead of the hull. How far had they been carried, they wondered. Where were they now? They all looked to Andrew Jack as he scanned the landmarks along the banks; then they saw his incredulous expression. Their eyes followed his pointing finger toward a tree and a stranded boat they had noticed the evening before, followed it back toward the sandbar they had passed, followed it toward Island Thirty-one. With him, they looked down at the water, at the hawser, still tight.

"The island's gone," he said hoarsely. "We're still where we were."

10

They had to cut the hawser; its invisible end was caught fast in the deep recesses of the mighty river, tied till its dissolution to a tree that might never again be seen. One piece of information they would surely have for Zadoc Cramer: Island Thirty-two was no more. They had presided at its obsequies.

The island's disappearance had shaken their newfound confidence. As they set off toward Flour Island five miles ahead, so named for the many flour boats wrecked there, and the Chickasaw Bluffs beyond, they felt awed once more by the power of the river and the earth and even more helpless as Jack declared himself hopelessly lost. Just past the Bluffs, those heights in which the veins of pink and yellow and blue were constantly exposed by the crumbling of the banks, they overtook a sixty-foot barge that was keeping to the swift current by dint of its long oars. Jack hailed it, calling to ask if the pilot knew where the channel was, but he professed himself as lost as they. "Jest stayin' where it looks like it oughta be!" he shouted, and that seemed to be all anyone could do.

To stay in the swift-flowing current was not without a special risk, for in the bends, where the rushing waters struck the shore and whirled around the curve and then glanced off to form a bend in the opposite direction, the deepest water was immediately under the bank, just where those trees undermined by the current were likely to fall outward into the water to smash whatever was passing beneath. Not only Andrew Jack and Nicholas studied what lay ahead; Lydia, too, and all the crew who were on deck watched tensely to spot any point on which the bank was crumbling, a tree about to fall.

But what they had been almost afraid to think was true: The tremors *were* growing weaker, and with each day's travel the damage along the shores was less. Gaps in the forests and cane brakes where earth had been torn away were fewer, and the birds ashore and on the wing sang once again and flew in familiar patterns. Still, though, the changes in the river and the burden it carried were evidence of violence past—and the earth still trembled. The crewmen felt it, going ashore for wood. They would work in what had become habitual silence, waiting. And when the sickening shudder came, they would pause with uplifted axes or set them quietly down on a log as though not to anger whatever spirit it was that moved the earth. Aboard the vessel, Lydia knew when the tremor was coming, for then Tiger would move toward her, moaning softly and trembling, as he laid his big head in her lap.

The racketing noise of logs hit by the wheels seemed never to stop; watery forests blocking the way brought out rowboat and axes and poles. At the Devil's Race Ground, that tangle of trees through which the river roared, above which John Bradbury stopped that fateful night, there seemed no way to penetrate the jungle, no space wide enough for even a flatboat, certainly no channel deep enough for them. But somehow they managed, with the men to clear ahead and with the marvelous synchronization between Baker and Jack, pilot and engineer, while all aboard waited tensely for the telltale scrape of hull against shoal or for a grinding crash. The steamboat snaked her way past the Devil's Elbow, a point formed by the river's sudden turning, where the channel was beset with snags at the best of times and where the former channel was no more. They chopped and pushed their way through rafts—wood islands of trees and driftwood and debris cast up from below by the river's rage—and worked the steamboat around and off new-formed sandbars unexpectedly blocking her path. When, at last, they reached one wonderfully long stretch in which the *New Orleans* steamed along at a steady nine miles an hour, all of them burst into the hysterical laughter of relief.

Progress was faster now. They wound their way past Paddy's Hens and Chickens, three islands in a bend, and past Fort Pickering, where they saw that the blockhouse had been damaged. And soon after passing Council Island (the name a memorial to those meetings at which the seizure of Indian lands was formalized), they began to see along the shore the camps of exhausted travelers, fugitives from the terrible ordeal upriver, who were taking time to assess damages to their boats and repair them for the remainder of their voyages. At the mouth of the St. Francis, where a number of vessels that had experienced the full terror of the earthquake were moored, the *New Orleans* stopped too. Not only were downriver voyagers here; so too were hunters and trappers from the interior who had brought their catch to the village for trade, and few came without some tale of damage or fright. Right here at the St. Francis, a severe shock had shaken the earth only two days earlier, on December 21, at half past four in the morning, and toppled some buildings. Travelers reported that the earth had trembled at Natchez and the river been violently convulsed, and a trapper who had brought his furs down the Washita River told of a mountain in the Arkansas region that was rent in two. Indian runners, it was said, brought word of log houses tumbled as far away as Georgia, and of rumblings beneath the earth far to the east and flashes of fire at sea.

Part of a day had to be spent in cleaning the boiler, full of mud and silt now, and in making minor repairs. During the delay, Nicholas invited those who would to come aboard to see the engine and the cabin, a marred cabin now but surely more elegant than any before seen in the region. The steamboat's arrival had created only a mild sensation—after an earthquake, the sense of wonder was dulled—but there were few who did not respond, *159* both the well-to-do merchants traveling aboard their vessels and the rivermen, instinctively hostile but curious, too, even a little envious as they saw that the crewmen of the *New Orleans* had to deal with neither oars nor sails.

With only a week of December left, they were four hundred miles from Natchez, six hundred from New Orleans. There was no hope of reaching the latter before the New Year, but Natchez they might. Pilots coming upriver reported that although the earth still trembled no major hindrances lay ahead, and as quickly as possible Nicholas ordered preparations for departure. All the wood that the *New Orleans* could carry was taken aboard, and what supplies were available from the small settlement store were bought to replenish their sadly depleted larder. Along the next three hundred miles lay only wilderness, with Chickasaw land on the east, and on the west the unsettled, flood-prone shores of the barren Louisiana Territory. Not until they reached the mouth of the Yazoo, where Mississippi Territory began, would scattered farms and villages promise that civilization lay ahead (if, as some doubted, civilization actually existed in the den of iniquity that was Natchez).

On the second day after leaving the St. Francis, the steamboat passed the mouth of the Arkansas, where a number of vessels were tied up, among them the barge on which John Bradbury was traveling. The *New Orleans* stopped here to wood up and to exchange a hail and what those aboard thought was a farewell but that would turn out not to be. John Bradbury would soon be in Natchez too; and there would board the steamboat to satisfy his curiosity about this "very handsome vessel . . . impelled by a very powerful steam engine."

Past bayous and rivers and islands they steamed, past brooding cypress swamps where Spanish Beard hung in great festoons, and past plantations set back within huge groves of oaks, where all the residents, black and white, came rushing to the bank to see the steamboat go by, their excitement a tonic as much to Lydia and Nicholas as to the crew. They saw the place where Stack Island had been and exclaimed; not only Island Thirty-two had disappeared! And then at last on the thirtieth of December they passed Island One Hundred Fourteen and Bayou Teche across from it and knew that it was time to move toward the left bank in preparation for rounding to and dropping into the eddy at the Natchez landing.

Natchez—first capital of the Mississippi Territory, boom-town, port of entry, health resort of sorts (Zadoc Cramer felt his consumption was being cured), cotton center—and city of sin. Built on a nearly perpendicular hill two hundred feet high, the town boasted aristocrats and beautiful homes, prosperous merchants and glittering parties, and (depending on who was boasting and to whom) the wildest, most sinful, roughest, most exciting area along the river, Natchez-under-the-Hill.

From upriver where the *New Orleans* had been sighted, riders had brought news of her approach. Crowds, thousands of people, were gathered on the bluff and at its foot. A band of Indians, hopeful of money or whisky, waited with home-made instruments to serenade the vessel's arrival. Planters and slaves and merchants and rivermen were there, many of them old friends or friends of friends. City officials stood waiting. Aboard the steamboat, excitement was intense. The children were dressed in their best, Nicholas stood erect and immaculately groomed in the bow, Lydia was breathing a prayer of thanks, and her pretty maid had stars in her eyes—Mr. Baker had just popped the question. They were all poised for the triumphant arrival, the dramatic sweep that would bring the *New Orleans* into full view.

The steamboat rounded to. Jack turned her head upstream to face the assembled crowd. Nicholas stood proud; the crew grinned, already savoring the sweet taste of success in a venture so many had said would fail. All of them, released from the fear and the terror of the days just past, were almost silent, so inadequate were the words they would say.

The *New Orleans* dropped back. And back. And *back!* She couldn't! Oh, she could not! There was consternation aboard, there were groans. After all she had been through, after her gallant, victorious battle—to be humiliated now? What was happening?

What was happening was that the river was having its bitter

joke. In one last defiant taunt, the current was carrying the steamboat far below the intended landing, out of control, while the expectant crowds on shore exclaimed, shook their heads, sighed. The skeptics nodded. You see! Oh, *down*stream, yes. . . . The steamboat's champions, chagrined, turned to one another, shrugging helplessly. In the bow of the boat, Lydia was almost crying as Nicholas swore shockingly, and practically leaped into the engine room, where Baker, in expectation of a stay of several days here (and perhaps in a lover's daze), had let the fires go down too low. All hands were ordered to heave to, to man the furnace; wood was snatched up, passed on, thrown into the fire; the flames rose, the chimney roared, smoke and burning chips poured from the stack. The engine was stopped so that steam could build up, and after what seemed hours but was less than one, the safety valve lifted, the steam hissed, Jack gave a few turns to the wheel to steady the boat, and at last, with only a slight edge missing from the zest of arrival, the approach to the landing resumed. From shore rose the wonderful, dreamed-about sound of cheers.

Landing took little time. The men were adept, and eagerness to be ashore sped them on. Then Lydia, leaving Henry with a radiant maid and holding Rosetta by the hand, stepped lightly ashore behind Nicholas as the cheers became a roar and around them crowded the privileged who had been given choice spots and lesser well-wishers too. Zadoc Cramer was there, coughing in the December cold but full of questions about the voyage and the river; so was Dr. Brown, whom they knew from their earlier voyage and who asked with interest what news they had of Colonel Burr. A number of Burr's "little band" had settled in Natchez after the failure of their coup. From all sides came a chorus of congratulations, sweet to Nicholas's ears. It was a great day for the West, he was told, thanks to his initiative. Steam was here to stay! The boat was a wonder. Mr. Samuel Davis, a cotton planter, announced to Mr. Roosevelt that he was planning to send a bale of cotton to New Orleans on the steamboat and was rewarded with one of Nicholas's rare smiles of pure delight. He would be the first, he was told, to venture a bale on such a risk!

While Nicholas talked to the men, Lydia was happy to see old friends and acquaintances. She reveled in their amazement at her courage in having her baby on the steamboat and ignored some disapproving glances, listened happily to their comments upon Henry's lustiness and Rosetta's charm, and still had time to remember the exciting secret she had just been told and the brilliant idea she herself had had.

During these harrowing days, all those aboard the *New Orleans* had grown close to one another. They had shared so much, seen pretenses vanish in the raw emotion of fear, come to know a mutual dependency. And now there was happiness to share. With some of the ladies Lydia held a quiet conference, and there were quick glances toward the young woman who stood at the end of the wharf holding Henry and talking with animation to Mr. Baker, the engineer, who had come ashore to bask in the begrudging admiration of the rivermen. Lydia offered a suggestion. The ladies responded with conspiratorial glee and two or three of them moved over toward the group of men gathered around Nicholas. As they whispered in their respective husbands' ears. All eyes turned toward the couple.

Going over to them and holding out her arms for Henry, Lydia laughed to see their wonder. Then, to those two whose romance had been born and flourished amid terror and tension and emotions that stripped character bare and must surely therefore endure, she presented her wonderful idea. They looked at each other, questioning. Baker murmured something and was answered with a joyous smile, a nod. Lydia waved, signaling to someone in the waiting group. A servant was dispatched with a message, and a little later, in the presence of a small party gathered on the steamboat and a large party watching from shore, the clergyman who had been sent for performed the first wedding ceremony ever held aboard a steamboat in the whole wide world.

Eleven days later, on January 10, 1812, the Place d'Armes in the city of New Orleans was alive with the movement of people crossing the square to the levee beyond. Along Chartres Street, where the great doors of the cathedral stood open for pious visiting, fashionably dressed women and gentlemen with walking canes were strolling toward the square; so were military men in uniform and black-cassocked clergy, slaves on household errands and free people of color, Indians in tribal dress, ships' captains, merchants from the Exchange, and visitors from the East and from Europe. The hum and buzz of conversation was, to the uninitiated, an incomprehensible mélange of languages and of innumerable accents drawn from Paris and London and Santo Domingo (whose refugees had almost doubled the city's population in the last five years), from Boston and parts of Africa and Cuba and Madrid.

From the Town House, delegates to the Constitutional Convention, who had been meeting to draw up a document for presentation this very month to the Congress of the United States with application for statehood, were emerging, greeting friends as they met them on their way to the square.

"Has the governor's carriage arrived?" was a repeated question.

"Yes, with Edward Livingston in it. He's very proprietary about his brother's boat."

"His brother's and Fulton's, you'd better say!"

"What about Roosevelt?"

"From what I hear, they are going to try to squeeze him out. Livingston says Fulton is furious—hasn't heard a word from Roosevelt, but plenty from his creditors in Pittsburgh."

"Hmm. They'll do it, too."

There had been those earthquakes upriver, though, someone said. They must have been pretty bad; it was remarkable that the vessel'd gotten through. Conversation turned to other matters. Had anyone heard the latest on war with England? There'd been another vessel boarded. John Randolph's speech was in the paper; he claimed it would be foolhardy to go to war under the ominous auspices of comets and earthquakes. Clay was urging war; so was Calhoun. By the way, someone said, the governor is appointing a committee to take a ride on the steamboat, see if she does what they claim.

As the strollers entered the square and looked toward the

The Mississippi at New Orleans. From *Forty Etchings, from Sketches Made with the Camera Lucida, in North America, in 1827 and 1828* by Basil Hall.

levee road, conversation turned to the immediate event. From here could be seen the elegant trotting horses, heads tossing, pulling the smart carriages of upriver planters along the levee road toward the spot at which Governor Claiborne would welcome the *New Orleans*. Some men were on horseback, cantering about showily before alighting to meet their carriage-borne wives, whose black servants helped them down and then mounted the carriages to be driven out of the way. At a respectful distance from the favored spot, other figures appeared atop the levee, farmers who had been hawking their produce in the market house below and trappers who had brought in game for the meat stalls, country people in from the bayous, curious strangers drawn by the excitement, drifters, tavern keepers, whores. Most of the sailors in town, in their striped shirts and buckskins, were already on the bank below.

In the embracing curve of the river, the masts of the ranked ships opposite the square peopled the sky, their rigging stretched among them like lace. Farther upstream, but still in the splendid crescent, the keelboats were moored, and farther on, the lowly flatboats, one after another; there were times when a man could walk for a mile from roof to roof. New Orleans, "mart of all the wealth of the western world," was a river metropolis, key to the western trade, an international port. A city of almost twenty thousand, half white, one quarter free colored and a quarter slave, French and Spanish in history, French in heart, and American now in name, a city where Catholic piety shrugged at secular fri- *165* volity and where voodoo chants echoed at night from Congo Square, where silken gowns (from France) rustled in magnolia'd patios, it existed not for its charm and more sordid delights but because here a mighty river offered a magnificent port and access to all the world. Here what happened on the river was everyone's concern.

From the deck of the *New Orleans,* where all the company was gathered save for the hands on duty below, the sight of the waterfront, with its hundreds of vessels, its beautiful curve, with the spires of the cathedral rising behind the distant square, in which the colorful dress of the people within made a whirling kaleidoscope, with the carriages drawn up on the levee and the crowd of dignitaries waiting to receive them, was so welcome, so beautiful, that for a moment no one spoke. Then Lydia turned toward Nicholas, smiling her delight. All had gone well since their stop in Natchez, as though the wedding so spontaneously arranged had symbolized a new beginning for their journey, too. A more concrete symbol was Mr. Samuel Davis's bale of cotton, first of many cargoes whose enormous profits even they could not foresee (nor, unfortunately, would they enjoy). Whatever auspices had shadowed the steamboat's voyage had turned into shining ones now.

As the *New Orleans* rounded to and moved toward the landing, those astonishing paddle wheels churning the muddy water and the smoke billowing from the stack and the steam floating out in clouds, curious sailors hung on nearby rigging to watch, while Governor Claiborne and others who had seen steamboats and even traveled on them in the East looked knowing and explained matters to those around them, and ordinary spectators gaped. They saw the paddle wheels gradually slow, hesitate, lift and fall, lift and fall, stop. They saw the crew tossing out lines that were hauled in by willing roustabouts on shore, eager to play some role in the arrival of this spectacular vessel. On the wharf, Governor Claiborne waited, resplendent in full ceremonial dress; aboard, Nicholas matched him in elegance (excelled him or anyone else, Lydia thought, in handsomeness).

The gangplank was lowered. The governor stepped forward.

(Why did Edward Livingston look so glum?) Then, for just an instant, before he advanced toward the long-awaited meeting, Lydia touched her husband's hand, felt his quick response. They had done it, together. Whatever lay ahead, whatever defeats (none, please God), whatever victories, this voyage had been their offering to the future. Other voyages would surely follow; other steamboats, finer, faster, would someday travel the western waters in a continuous parade, carrying people, cargoes, dreams, even a nation's destiny, but theirs had been the first, showing the way. Proudly Lydia looked after Nicholas.

She'd like to hear what Papa would have to say now!

EPILOGUE

Papa had lots to say. Until he himself became a victim of Fulton's ruthlessness, he supported the criticism of Roosevelt, writing many an "I told you so" to his son-in-law. Only later would he recognize that Roosevelt had his own just grievances and become friend instead of critic once again.

The Roosevelts remained in New Orleans for several months after the steamboat's arrival, Roosevelt acting as agent for the Ohio Steamboat Navigation Company until relations with Fulton became intolerable. During the following years, he was involved in a dizzying succession of projects, from inventing an engine run by gunpowder to founding his own steamboat company in Shrewsbury, New Jersey, from planning a water system for the city of Nashville to taking shares in whatever projects looked interesting—waterworks, steamboats, land development. In 1813, he managed to pay off the Navy debt, either by pledging land or declaring insolvency (the record is not clear). Debt continued, nevertheless, to dog his erratic footsteps. It rarely bothered him or apparently anyone else, save his creditors and Latrobe. When he was sued in Pittsburgh for debts contracted during the building of the *New Orleans,* the hearing was notable for a eulogy of

Lydia Latrobe Roosevelt (1791–1878). From the Nicholas Roosevelt Collection.

Mr. and Mrs. Roosevelt, delivered by the principal witness for the prosecution. In 1814, he was awarded the coveted patent for the side wheels, but in 1828 was too poor, or claimed to be, to press a suit attacking infringements upon it. Perhaps he simply recognized the suit's futility; beneath the relentless churning of paddle wheels, exclusive rights had been falling like jackstraws.

Whatever their financial status, Lydia and Nicholas evidently lived in comfort and great happiness, principally in New York City. Seven more children brought them respectably close to the standards of the times. Not until 1839, when he was seventy-two, did Nicholas retire, moving with his family to Skaneateles, New York. There, according to local chroniclers, he

Nicholas J. Roosevelt (1767–1854). From the Nicholas Roosevelt Collection.

settled down in "modest affluence," becoming at once a leading citizen. He is described by them as "a gentleman of the old school, courtly and dignified." "I used to like to see him," wrote one old-time resident, "with his long Dutch pipe, placidly enjoying an after dinner smoke."

Placidly? Nicholas? It is almost impossible to reconcile so tranquil a picture with that of the volatile, harum-scarum younger man—and not so young even then—who with a courageous young woman challenged the wicked river to do its darndest against him. And won.

Rich or poor, placid or not, Nicholas Roosevelt left his countrymen a legacy. After that epic voyage, the transportation revolution that would decide America's course for years to come was firmly launched. Experiments already under way were accelerated; others were begun. Within a decade, the steamboat had become an instrument of national progress and unity, propelling a young and vigorous people in the direction of their Manifest Destiny.

NOTES

Chapter 1

1   the twentieth day of October, 1811:   "The steam Boat sailed from this place on Sunday last, for the Natchez." *Pittsburgh Gazette*, Friday, Oct. 25, 1811. The statement contradicts that of J. H. B. Latrobe (*First Voyage*, p. 13) that the steamboat left Pittsburgh "in the latter part of September," a date totally unsupportable by evidence. More surprisingly, Robert Fulton seems to have been misled about the date of departure. "So that it has cost 10688.35 to work the Boat from Pittsburgh from which she started the 16 of Oct. to May 4th, 6 months ½." Letter to John Livingston in New Orleans, June 15, 1812. Roosevelt Family Papers in the Franklin D. Roosevelt Library, Hyde Park, N.Y.

2   Mississippi Steamboat Navigation Company: The Mississippi Company and the Ohio Steamboat Navigation Company, both organized by Robert Fulton and Robert Livingston, are often confused. The first was established in 1809 (Talbot Hamlin, *Benjamin Henry Latrobe*, New York, 1955, p. 372) and built all of the Fulton-Livingston vessels destined for the Mississippi. The Ohio Steamboat Navigation Company, chartered by the state of Indiana in 1810, built vessels only for the Ohio. Louis C. Hunter, *Steamboats on the Western Rivers*, Cambridge, 1949, pp. 309–10.

2   she loomed large: The measurements of the *New Orleans*, like her appearance, are uncertain. Those given here are from Hunter (*Steamboats*, p. 77), whose authority is popularly accepted. His source, however, was John Melish (*Travels in the United States of America*, Philadelphia, 1812, vol. II, p. 60), who saw the vessel on the stocks but gave no source for his figures. Contemporary authorities equally reliable, like Zadoc Cramer (*The Navigator*, Pittsburgh, 1814) and the *Pittsburgh Gazette* of Oct. 18, 1811, give somewhat different ones. Tonnage was at least 400 tons. Official report to Governor W. C. C. Claiborne, Jan. 19, 1812, in the *Territorial Papers of the United States*, vol. 9, *The Territory of Orleans, 1803–1812*, Washington, 1940; and William C. Bradbury, *Travels in the Interior of America*, 1809–1811, in *Early Western Travels, 1748–1846*, ed. Reuben Gold Thwaites, vol. V, p. 211, Cleveland, 1904. The original plans, not extant, seem to have been for a 116-foot hull with a 20-foot beam. John H. B. Latrobe, *The First Steamboat Voyage on the Western Waters*, Baltimore, 1871, pp. 11–12.

2   her little girl: The existence of Rosetta Mark Roosevelt, born Jan. 31, 1810 (m. John Fitch. Charles Barney Whittelsey, *The Roosevelt Genealogy*, Hartford, 1902. Addenda to p. 40 and p. 54) has been ignored almost completely by chroniclers of the voyage. Roosevelt left Pittsburgh with "his little family" (Charles J. Latrobe, *The Rambler in North America*, London, 1835, vol. I., p. 105), with his wife pregnant "for the second time." J. H. B. Latrobe, *First Voyage*, pp. 19–20. Mention of her presence in Pittsburgh prior to the voyage and in New Orleans immediately after gives further evidence that she accompanied her parents. B.H.L. to Lydia, Dec. 18, 1810; to Jacob Mark, Nov. 5, 1811; to Lydia, Jan. 17, 1812. Lacking any firsthand account of the child's activities on the voyage, her role can be based only on indirect evidence.

7   ideal of the "lady":   Arthur W. Calhoun, *A Social History of the American Family*, New York, 1945; Mary Sumner Benson, *Women in Eighteenth Century America*, New York, 1935; Elizabeth Anthony Dexter, *Career Women of America, 1776–1840*, Francestown, N.H., 1950. According to these observers and others, female independence declined as national independence increased.

8   had many local connections: It is continually astonishing to stumble across the web of family, social, and political ties that bound together early citizens of the republic. Alexis de Tocqueville commented that "all the able men in the Union know each other by reputation, many of them personally." *Journey to America*, New Haven, 1960,

p. 271. Letters of introduction such as the Roosevelts carried (Latrobe, *First Voyage,* p. 7) would have made it virtually impossible for them not to know everyone of consequence in Pittsburgh.

11 "scarcely imagine . . . a boat . . .":   Timothy Flint, *Recollections of the Last Ten Years,* Boston, 1826; republished by Da Capo Press, New York, 1968, p. 14.

13 New England . . . might well secede: Josiah Quincy, in a speech to the House on Jan. 14, 1811. *Debates,* 11 Congress, 3 Session, pp. 524–42. Arguments for the sovereignty of states and the legitimacy of secession prior to the Hartford Convention of 1814 contained all the elements out of which Jefferson Davis and John C. Calhoun constructed their nullification and secession doctrines. "A Forgotten Phase of the New England Opposition to the War of 1812," by Frank Maloy Anderson in *Proceedings of the Mississippi Valley Historical Association,* vol. VI, 1912–13, pp. 176–188, Torch Press, Cedar Rapids, Iowa. 1913.

13 " . . . formed into one stream":   In a letter to Charles Pinckney, Minister to Spain, Nov. 27, 1802. Printed in American State Papers. *Foreign Affairs,* vol. II, p. 527.

14 the same monopoly: Fulton had grandiose ambitions. In 1811 he was seeking from the Russian czar the exclusive privilege of running steamboats between St. Petersburg and Kronstadt, and in the following year entered into an agreement with an Englishman to introduce steamboats on the Ganges. Hunter, *Steamboats,* p. 9.

15 nagging sense of injustice: Claimants to priority in the use of side-wheels are several. Testimony suggests that John Fitch tried out a boat with side paddle wheels on Collect Pond in 1796 or 1797 and that his experiment was witnessed by Robert Livingston and possibly Nicholas Roosevelt. In 1798 Samuel Morey of Orford, N.H., constructed a steamboat with paddle wheels at the side, which was propelled to Philadelphia and publicly exhibited. Roosevelt's grievance is given special validity, however, by his connection with Livingston. See. J. H. B. Latrobe, *A Lost Chapter in the History of the Steamboat,* Baltimore, 1871.

16 Great Comet of 1811:   The Great Comet of 1811, one of the most celebrated of modern times, was visible for seventeen months, from March 26, 1811, when it was sighted at Viviers, France, to August 17, 1812, when it was last seen at Neu-Tscherkask in the south of Russia. Sir William Herschel estimated the diameter of the nucleus to be 428 miles, the real length of the tail upwards of one hundred *175*

million miles, with a breadth of fifteen million. Astronomers have assigned to it a period of three thousand and sixty-five years. George F. Chambers, *The Story of the Comets*, Oxford, at the Clarendon Press, 1909, pp. 129–31.

17   "I wish Lydia were the husband!":   *Papers of Benjamin Henry Latrobe* ed. Edward C. Carter II, Maryland Historical Society, 1976, letter of Feb. 23, 1812.

18   a year of omens: C. J. Latrobe, *The Rambler in North America*, vol. I, pp. 105–7.

Chapter 2

25   an angry mob of Philadelphia citizens: Roosevelt's stormy relations with the city of Philadelphia in connection with the waterworks project are recounted in Talbot Hamlin's *Benjamin Henry Latrobe*, pp. 170–77 passim. In trying to force acceptance of his terms for the sale of his lease on the subsidiary rolling mill, he turned off the water for three hours and was blamed for the spread of a serious fire in the city. Soon thereafter he threatened to blow up the engines unless his asking price was accepted. When the Council secured a writ against him, Roosevelt locked the gates against the sheriff, who, with the help of angry citizens, broke open the locks and threw out Roosevelt and his men. There is some evidence that he had other serious legal troubles. Latrobe's *Lost Chapter* makes veiled reference to Roosevelt's having been imprisoned for debt (p. 33).

26   "wondrous ships . . . ":   *The Iliad*, VIII, ll. 556–58.

27   granted a patent: The patent is dated Dec. 1, 1814, and is signed by James Madison, President; James Monroe, Secretary of State; and Richard Rush, Attorney General.

27   Patent suits: The Battle of the Patents, as it came to be known, continued among various claimants for years. It was effectively concluded by the decision of the Supreme Court in *Gibbons* vs. *Ogden* in 1824 annulling the Fulton-Livingston franchise.

28   "fire engines":   There are many histories of the invention of the steamboat. James T. Flexner, *Steamboats Come True*, gives a most interesting survey of its development, especially in America, focusing on the personalities and struggles of its inventors. Louis C. Hunter's authoritative *Steamboats on the Western Rivers* is an economic and technological history.

29   Fitch, a country bumpkin: Flexner's evidence for Franklin's shab-

by treatment of Fitch is convincing. *Steamboats,* pp. 95, 145–58 passim. Franklin, says Flexner, considered Fitch "a grotesque fool," p. 370.

30 most critical of his relatives: According to B.H. Latrobe, Roosevelt was often "at variance" with his relatives. Letter to Lydia, Dec. 18, 1810. Except for an early land purchase, none of his relatives seem to have been associated with him in business projects. No family names appear on mortgages or deeds signed by him.

30 a double-acting engine: The patent for this reciprocating steam engine is in the Roosevelt Library at Hyde Park.

32 wheels over the side: Letter from Livingston to Roosevelt, Oct. 28, 1798. Included in Latrobe's *Lost Chapter,* p. 35.

32 "a most inveterate schemer . . . ": B.H.L. letter to son Henry, Feb. 21, 1813.

32 " . . . a powerful figure . . . ": Nicholas Roosevelt, *A Front Row Seat,* Norman, Okla., 1953, p. 6.

34 steam engines . . . "subject to casualties . . . ": *Philadelphia Gazette,* July 31, 1800.

35 mortgaged his engine works: Although Latrobe had the original contract, Roosevelt evidently dealt directly with the city of Philadelphia in connection with his engines. The city held his mortgage until 1806. It also advanced sums to him on his notes, which were endorsed by Latrobe. Hamlin, *Latrobe,* pp. 171–73.

36 " . . . our esteem . . . ": Nov. 2, 1804.

36 "Were you really serious?": to Roosevelt, Nov. 23, 1804.

37 " . . . better to laugh": to Roosevelt, Dec. 17, 1804.

37 " . . . as affected as a Cat . . . ": April 16, 1805, to his brother Christian.

42 became a partner: Hamlin, *Latrobe,* p. 372.

Chapter 3

49 a fee . . . of twenty-five cents: *History of the Panhandle, Wheeling, W. Va.,* compiled by Newton, Nichols, and Sprankle, in Ethel C. Leahy, *Who's Who on the Ohio River,* Cincinnati, 1931, p. 311.

51 " . . . a novel sight": *The Navigator,* 1811, 14, p. 30.

51 the paddle wheels: Roosevelt's patent application (1814) and let-

ter to Livingston of Sept. 6, 1798 (*Lost Chapter*, p. 35) describe the mechanism.

52   Sixty to eighty . . . passengers: No plans for the first *New Orleans* have been discovered. Based on accommodations provided on other Fulton vessels and contemporary steamboats, the main cabin could have been fifty or more feet in length, accommodating perhaps fifty passengers in its narrow, shelflike berths. Deck passengers were expected to find what space they could on deck amid machinery and cargo.

54   every detail of the voyage: The incidents of the flatboat voyage are recounted in *The First Steamboat Voyage*, pp. 7–11 passim, in scattered letter references, and in a letter from B. H. Latrobe to Fulton, Feb. 1, 1813, appealing for consideration of Roosevelt's rights to his portion of the steamboat's profits and the assignment of them to his wife and her heirs.

56   the Indian Queen: Alexander B. Adams, *John James Audubon*, New York, 1966, p. 89.

58   "Her appearance . . . elegant . . . ":   *Western Spectator*, Nov. 11, 1811.

58   number of children: *The Navigator*, 1814, p. 85.

58   her scrawly handwriting: Benjamin Henry Latrobe, *Journals, 1799–1820*, New Haven, 1980, p. 56. Latrobe makes the same comparison between Aaron Burr's handwriting and that of his father, whom he never knew.

59   Point Pleasant: Archer B. Hulbert, *The Ohio River*, New York, 1906, pp. 332 ff.

59   the pillory: Cramer, *The Navigator*. Cramer frequently deplores the continuing use of the pillory and the whipping post in Virginia, e.g., re Charlestown: "What a pity that an enlightened people, in an enlightened age should use such a disgraceful, inhuman, and savage machinery of punishment." Edition of 1817, p. 79.

61   making her dignified appearance: Letter of July 9, 1862, in the Orlando Brown Papers, the Filson Club, Louisville, Ky.

Chapter 4

64   " . . . a drop of white blood . . . ":   Tecumseh spoke these words to Louis de Mun of St. Louis. Latrobe, *Journals*, New York, 1905, p. 75. Eloquent, courageous, and inspired, Tecumseh organized wide-

spread resistance to the white man's advances in company with his brother, the Prophet, whom the tribes held in superstitious awe. Tecumseh was commissioned a brigadier general in the British Army at the outbreak of the War of 1812 and was killed in the battle of the Thames, Oct. 5, 1813.

67   she'd complained about: Letter from Lucy Audubon to cousin Euphemia Gifford, May 27, 1808. L. Clark Keating, *Audubon, The Kentucky Years*, Lexington, 1976, p. 25.

71   were stopping in Louisville: A letter from Audubon to his friend Ferdinand Rozier (Nov. 2, 1811) states that he and his family reached Louisville October 31 and were staying for two or three days on their way to Pennsylvania. Francis Hobart Herrick, *Audubon the Naturalist*, 2 vols., New York, 1968, vol. I, p. 243. The chronology disproves the popular local legend that when the *New Orleans* stopped at Henderson Audubon dived under the bow and came up at the stern. He *could* have done so at Louisville.

71   Henry Shreve: That Shreve visited the steamboat at Louisville is accepted by his biographers and others. Florence Dorsey, *Master of the Mississippi*, New York, 1941; Stirling North, *The First Steamboat Voyage on the Mississippi*, Boston, 1962. The dates of his upriver trip place him in Louisville during the steamboat's stay there. With his own steamboat plans already under way, he would hardly have missed inspecting the *New Orleans*.

72   " . . . of smelling the first powder . . . ":   *Liberty Hall*, Oct. 30, 1811.

73   Halley: *Kentucky Gazette*, Oct. 15, 1811.

77   Frequent experiments: *Liberty Hall*, Nov. 21, 1811.

79   "Will our government act . . . ?":   Letter to the editor of the *Western Courier* (Louisville), Nov. 8, 1811, in *Liberty Hall*, Nov. 21, 1811.

Chapter 5

86   court-appointed pilot: Because the Kentucky state line extended to the low water mark on the Indiana shore, Kentucky could license pilots for the Indian Chute.

87   all the steam it could bear: In the opinion of many rivermen, the low-pressure engine had inadequate reserve power for the difficult western waters. Because the capacity of the condenser is constant, an increase in steam pressure brings no increase in power. When more

steam than can be condensed by the water spray enters the condenser, the increased pressure on the driving side of the piston is largely offset by the incomplete vacuum obtained on the other side. Hunter, *Steamboats*, pp. 130–32. Evidently Baker and other early engineers did not agree.

90   six cords of wood: J.G. Flügel, *Journal of a Voyage, Louisiana Historical Quarterly*, July 1924, p. 433. The boiler from the first *New Orleans* was used in the second, on which Flügel was a passenger.

91   had not been one in over a year: Letter from Eliza Bryan, in *History of Cosmopolite, or the Writings of Rev. Lorenzo Dow*, Cincinnati, 1849, p. 344.

92   They left . . . Friday: From Shippingport to the mouth of the Ohio, few precise details of the steamboat's progress are accessible. Only one landing is documented. Dates given are estimates, based upon the vessel's probable speed, the prevailing preferences in landing places, and correlation with recorded events and experiences.

92   Territory, largely barren: The notion that fertile land lay to the west did not develop for many years. William Brackenridge, who explored the Louisiana Territory in 1810–12, compared it to the Sahara or Tartary. Except for a belt of 150 to 200 miles in width along the rivers, he wrote, the province of Louisiana (all of middle America) was "little more than a barren waste." Henry M. Brackenridge, *Views of Louisiana*, Pittsburgh, 1814, p. 67.

Chapter 6

97   Audubon described them: Maria R. Audubon, *Audubon and His Journals*, New York, 1897, p. 107.

98   its name, *Ohio:*   Hulbert, *The Ohio River*, New York, 1806, pp. 2–4. According to Hulbert, the Indian name was represented by *Oyo*, with *oyoneri* an adverbial form of beautiful in Onondaga. In Miami dialect, *O'hui* or *Ohi* meant instead "very," as in *Ohiopeek*, "very white." The river was called *Ohiopeekhanne*, the "white foaming river," for the white caps frequently seen in the Miami area.

104   coal, already quarried, lay: C.J. Latrobe, *The Rambler*, vol. I, p. 106.

107   the main stream: Many considered the Missouri the main stream. Zadoc Cramer called it "in fact the principal river." *Navigator*, 1817,

p. 133. John Melish pointed out that it extended 1670 miles, while the Mississippi, without it, extended only 730, less than such "tributaries" as the Red River and the Arkansas and the Platte. *Geographical Description,* p. 30. The source of the Mississippi was not discovered until 1832, when its discoverer, Henry Rowe Schoolcraft, named the mother lake in northern Minnesota *Itasca.*

Chapter 7

111   the rift remained: Study of the rift and related faults in the New Madrid area became possible only in the last decade, with the development by the oil industry of sophisticated deep-sounding equipment. During 1978–79, scientists from the United States Geological Survey, from St. Louis University, from the Midwest Research Institute in Kansas City, and from other study centers carried on seismic reflection profiling that revealed much of the configuration of deep rock strata in the region. The findings explain seismic activity that has long puzzled scientists by reason of its occurrence in the middle of the North American crustal plate, where friction should not occur. "Recurrent Intraplate Tectonism in the New Madrid Seismic Zone," M.D. Zoback, R.M. Hamilton, et al., *Science* Magazine, Aug. 29, 1980, pp. 971–76; "Quakes Along the Mississippi," Robert M. Hamilton, *Natural History,* Aug. 1980, pp. 70–75; *Time,* Nov. 19, 1979, pp. 66–67.

113   the earth convulsed: Description of the earthquake's immediate effects is taken from firsthand accounts by John Bradbury, *Travels in the Interior of America in the Years 1809, 1810, and 1811,* in Reuben Thwaites, *Early Western Travels,* vol. V, pp. 205–11; L. Bringier, *Notices of the Geology of the Regions around the Mississippi and its Confluent Waters* in a letter to Rev. Elias Cornelius, in the *American Journal of Science and Arts,* 1821, vol. III, p. 15; Eliza Bryan, in *History of Cosmopolite, or the Writings of Rev. Lorenzo Dow,* 7th ed., pp. 344–46; Godfrey Le Sieur, Letter to A.D. Hagar, former State Geologist of Missouri, in Campbell's *Gazetteer of Missouri,* St. Louis, 1874, p. 394; James McBride, "Down the Mississippi" in the Quarterly Publication of the *Historical and Philosophical Society of Ohio,* vol. V, no. 1, Jan.–March, 1910; William Leigh Pierce et al., *An Account of the Great Earthquake in the Western States, Particularly in the Mississippi River, December 16–23, 1811, Collected from Facts,* Newburyport, 1812; Col. John Shaw, *New Madrid Earthquake,* in the second annual *Report and Collections of the State Historical Society of Wisconsin for 1855,* reprinted in *Missouri Historical Review,* Columbia, Mo., Jan. 1912, p. 91.

117 " . . . to guard against anticipated attacks . . . ":   William Leigh
Pierce, *An Account*, p. 4.

125 Not only islands vanished: Descriptions of the earthquake's dev-
astating effects were given by later visitors to the area, some of them
such astute observers as Sir Charles Lyell, eminent British geologist.
Among those who recorded their findings were Michael Brounm, account of the Earthquake in *History of Dunklin County Missouri, 1845–
1895*, by Mary F. Smythe-Davis, p. 15; Timothy Flint, *Recollections
of the Last Ten Years in the Mississippi Valley*, Boston, 1826, p. 22;
J.W. Foster, *The Mississippi Valley: Its Physical Geography*, Chicago,
1869, p. 18; Sir Charles Lyell, *Second Visit to the United States of North
America*, New York, Harper & Bros., 1849, vol. II, p. 172. Fermin
A. Rozier, Report on the Submerged Lands of Missouri in *The Proceedings of the Southwestern Convention at Memphis, 1845* (also found in
the *Western Journal*, St. Louis, 1850, vol. III, p. 391); Lewis F. Linn,
Letter relative to the Obstructions to the Navigation of the White,
Big Black, at St. Francois (to the United States Senate), Feb. 1, 1836
(copied in Wetmore's *Gazetteer*).

126 new creeks were made: Michael Brounm, Account given in *History of Dunklin County, Mo., 1845–1895*, p. 15.

126 Reelfoot Lake: Michael Brounm, *Account . . . in History of Dunklin
County*, p. 15; Eliza Bryan, *Letter in History of Cosmopolite*, p. 345; Lewis F. Linn, *Letter . . . in* Wetmore, *Gazetteer*, p. 131. Testimony as
to the lake's dimensions varied, but by all accounts it was close to
those given. Over a period of almost two centuries, the lake has been
filled and silted in and now measures approximately 3 miles by 20.

126 speculating on the causes: "Earthquakes in Missouri", by Francis
A. Sampson, in *Proceedings of the Mississippi Valley Historical Association
for the Year 1912–1913*, ed. Benjamin F. Shambaugh, Torch Press,
Cedar Rapids, Iowa, 1913, vol. VI, pp. 233–35.

126 "given a small shake . . . ":   *Louisiana Gazette*, Dec. 21, 1811.

Chapter 8

129 like we're grounded: *First Voyage*, p. 23.

131 Americans attacked their food: Foreign visitors, shocked by
American table manners in general, were appalled at the conversation-
less wolfing at meals, the "bestial feeding" evident on steamboats. The
incessant spitting disturbed Mrs. Trollope. "I would infinitely prefer

sharing the apartment of a party of well-conditioned pigs to the being confined to its [the steamboat's] cabin," she wrote. *Domestic Manners of the Americans*, London: Whittaker, Treacher & Co., New York: reprinted 1832. vol I, p. 20.

133   fled into the woods: *Henderson,* American Guide Series, Bacon, Percy & Daggett, Northport, N.Y., 1941, p. 31.

137   canoes passed in and out: *First Voyage,* p. 24.

Chapter 9

144   Fire . . .!:   Fire, especially from explosion, was the most feared of all steamboat hazards. It was responsible for 1330 of the 1921 recorded fatalities from steamboat accidents in the United States before 1840. Hunter, *Steamboats,* p. 278. Although snagging caused greater property damage, fire usually meant hideous and spectacular death. Most steamboats had only a single yawl, lifeboats were unknown, few persons were able to swim, and the usually combustible cargo—hay, packing straw, oil, whisky, cotton, even gunpowder—encouraged a fire's spread. Graphic accounts of the results were given in newspaper accounts and such books as James T. Lloyd's *Lloyd's Steamboat Directory and Disasters on the Western Waters,* which described people "scorched and burned to a crisp," "literally roasted." The massive toll inspired artists to dramatic portrayals and the public to cries of protest. Congress was finally stirred to action, but no effective safety regulations were put into effect until 1852. Hunter, *Steamboats,* pp. 520–46.

148   Island Number Ten: Cramer, *The Navigator,* 1814; Eliza Bryan, in *History of Cosmopolite,* p. 346.

149   leaning *upstream:*   McBride, "Down the Mississippi," p. 28.

152   would not stop at New Madrid: *First Voyage,* p. 26.

156   "The island's gone":   *First Voyage,* p. 30; C.J. Latrobe, *The Rambler,* vol. I, p. 106; Cramer, *The Navigator,* 1817, p. 164.

Chapter 10

157   Just past the Bluffs: Daily progress and interim stops between New Madrid and Natchez are not recorded and cannot be positively determined. The itinerary proposed most reasonably accords with the testimony of other travelers along the river in the quake's

aftermath, with the steamboat's probable speed along changed and disrupted channels, and with the need for frequent refueling.

159 shock . . . at half past four: Bradbury, *Travels,* in Thwaite, *Western Travels,* p. 210.

160 "very handsome vessel . . . ":   Bradbury, *Travels,* p. 211.

162 to venture a bale: *Lost Chapter,* p. 34n.

163 first wedding ceremony: *First Voyage,* p. 32n.

164 Edward Livingston: Edward Livingston, the chancellor's much younger brother, was mayor of New York City in 1803 but moved to Louisiana the following year because of a financial scandal in the district attorney's office during his tenure. He eventually repaid the government and became a prominent lawyer, legislator, and statesman. He also became a beneficiary of the success of the *New Orleans,* becoming part owner of other boats built by the Mississippi Steamboat Navigation Company. His cousin, John Livingston, Fulton's brother-in-law, was put in charge of building those boats.

164 John Randolph's speech: *Louisiana Gazette,* Feb. 11, 1812.

165 a mile from roof to roof: Leland D. Baldwin, *The Keelboat Age on Western Waters,* Pittsburgh, 1941, p. 189.

166 enormous profits: In the 1814 *Navigator* and subsequent editions, Cramer noted that in the first year of the steamboat's operation the owners cleared over and above expenses, repairs, and interest $20,000 on a capital investment of $40,000. This revenue, he remarked, was "superior to [that of] any other establishment in the United States." As the word spread, steamboat building progressed at a feverish pace, fulfilling Cramer's prediction that enterprising westerners would "ere long, have steam boats of all sizes and fashions, running up and down our numerous rivers." The transportation revolution had begun.

SOURCE MATERIAL

Manuscripts

Orlando Brown Papers. The Filson Club, Louisville, Ky.

Robert Fulton Papers. New York Historical Society, New York, N.Y.

Benjamin Henry Latrobe Papers. Maryland Historical Society, Baltimore, Md. Microfiche copy in possession of Tulane University Library, New Orleans, La.

Robert R. Livingston Papers. New York Historical Society, New York, N.Y.

Livingston Family Papers. Franklin D. Roosevelt Library, Hyde Park, N.Y.

Roosevelt Family Papers. Franklin D. Roosevelt Library, Hyde Park, N.Y.

Newspapers

Cincinnati (Ohio) *Liberty Hall*
Cincinnati (Ohio) *Western Spy*
Frankfort (Ky.) *Palladium*
Lexington (Ky.) *Kentucky Gazette*
Marietta (Ohio) *Western Spectator*
Natchez (Miss.) *Gazette*
New Orleans (La.) *Louisiana Gazette*
New Orleans (La.) *Louisiana Courier*
Pittsburgh (Pa.) *Gazette*
Richmond (Va.) *Richmond Enquirer*

Other Printed Sources (Primary Materials)

Ashe, Thomas. *Travels in America, Performed in 1806.* London: R. Phillips, 1808.

Brackenridge, Henry M. *Views of Louisiana.* Pittsburgh: Cramer, Spear & Eichbaum, 1814.

Bradbury, John. *Travels in the Interior of America, in the Years 1809, 1810, and 1811,* in Reuben G. Thwaites, ed., *Early Western Travels,* vol. V. Cleveland: Arthur H. Clark Co., 1904.

Bringier, L. "Notices of the Geology of the Regions around the Mississippi and its Confluent Waters," *American Journal of Science and Arts,* 1821, vol. III, p. 15.

Brounm, Michael. Account of the Earthquake in *History of Dunklin County, Missouri, 1845–1895,* by Mary F. Smythe-Davis, p. 15.

Bryan, Eliza. Letter to the Rev. Lorenzo Dow, in *History of Cosmopolite, or the Writings of Rev. Lorenzo Dow,* 7th ed., Cincinnati, 1849.

Official Letter Books of W.C.C. Claiborne, 1801–1816, ed. Dunbar Rowland. Jackson, Miss.: State Department of Archives and History, 1917.

Cramer, Zadoc. *The Navigator: Containing Directions for Navigating the Monongahela, Alleghany, Ohio, and Mississippi Rivers,* edition of 1814, reprinted in part in Ethel C. Leahy, *Who's Who on the Ohio River.* Cincinnati: Ethel C. Leahy Pub. Co., 1931. Also Pittsburgh, edition of 1817.

Cumings, Samuel. *The Western Pilot, Containing Charts of the Ohio River, and of the Mississippi from the Mouth of the Missouri to the Gulf of Mexico.* Cincinnati, 1825.

Flint, Timothy. *Recollections of the Last Ten Years.* Boston, 1826; New York: Da Capo Press, 1868.

Flügel, J.G. "Pages from a Journal of a Voyage down the Mississippi to New Orleans in 1817," ed. Felix Flügel. *Louisiana Historical Quarterly,* Louisiana Historical Society, July, 1924, pp. 413–439.

Forman, S.S. *Narrative of a Journey down the Ohio and Mississippi in 1789–90.* Cincinnati: R. Clarke & Co., 1888.

Foster, John W. *The Mississippi Valley: Its Physical Geography.* Chicago: S.C. Griggs & Co., 1869.

Hall, Basil. *Forty Etchings, from Sketches Made with the Camera Lucida, in North America, in 1827 and 1828.* Edinburgh, 1829.

Hall, James. *Letters from the West.* London: H. Colborn, 1828.

Hildreth, Samuel P. *History of an Early Voyage on the Ohio and Mississippi Rivers, with Historical Sketches,* in *The American Pioneer,* Chillicothe, Ohio, 1842.

Latrobe, Benjamin Henry. *Journal.* New York: D. Appleton & Co., 1905.

Latrobe, Charles J. *The Rambler in North America,* vol. I (of 2). London: R.B. Seeley and W. Burnside, 1835.

Latrobe, John H.B. *The First Steamboat Voyage on the Western Waters.* Maryland Historical Society: Fund Publication No. 6, Baltimore, 1871.

Le Sieur, Godfrey. "Letter to A.D. Hagar, Former State Geologist of Missouri" in Campbell's *Gazetteer of Missouri*. St. Louis: R.A. Campbell, 1874.

Livingston, Robert R. "The Invention of the Steamboat." A letter from Chancellor Livingston to the editors of the *American Medical and Philosophical Register*, vol. II, Jan. 1812, p. 256. Boston: Directors of the Old South Work, 1902.

Lyell, Sir Charles. *Second Visit to the United States of North America*. New York: Harper & Bros., 1849.

Melish, John. *Geographical Description of the United States*. New York: A.T. Goodrich, 1826.

McBride, James. "Down the Mississippi," *Quarterly Publication of the Historical and Philosophical Society of Ohio*. vol. V, no. 1, Jan.–March, 1910, pp. 27–31.

Pierce, William Leigh et al. *An Account of the Great Earthquake in the Western States, Particularly in the Mississippi River, December 16–23, 1811. Collected from Facts*. Newburyport, 1812.

Rozier, Fermin A. "Report on the Submerged Lands of Missouri," in *Proceedings of the Southwestern Convention at Memphis*, 1845.

Rozier, Fermin A. *History of the Early Settlement of the Mississippi Valley*. St. Louis: G.A. Pierrot & Son, 1890. Contains accounts of the earthquake given by Lewis F. Linn, Letter relative to the Obstructions to the Navigation of the White, Big Black, at St. Francois (to the United States Senate), February 1, 1836; by John James Audubon, *Journal*, and Godfrey Le Sieur.

Shaw, Col. John. "New Madrid Earthquake," in the second annual *Report and Collections of the State Historical Society of Wisconsin*, 1855.

Schultz, Christian, Jr. *Travels on an Inland Voyage . . . in the Years 1807 and 1808*. New York: Isaac Riley, 1810.

Secondary Materials

Audubon, Maria. *Audubon and His Journals*. New York: Charles Scribner's Sons, 1897.

Adams, Alexander. *John James Audubon*, New York: G.P. Putnam's Sons, 1966.

Baldwin, Leland. *The Keelboat Age on Western Waters*. University of Pittsburgh Press, 1941.

Baldwin, Leland. *Pittsburgh: The Story of a City*. University of Pittsburgh Press, 1937.

Bogardus, Carl. *The First Steamboat Voyage on the Western Waters*. Austin, Indiana: The Muscatatuck Press, 1961.

Buck, Solon J., and Elizabeth H. *The Planting of Civilization in Western Pennsylvania.* University of Pittsburgh Press, 1939.

Chambers, George F. *The Story of the Comets.* Oxford: Clarendon Press, 1909.

Blair, Walter, and Franklin J. Meine. *Mike Fink, King of Mississippi Keelboatmen.* New York: 1933.

Churchill, Allen. *The Roosevelts: American Aristocrats.* New York: Harper & Row, 1965.

Dickinson, Henry W. *Robert Fulton.* London: John Lane, New York: John Lane Co., 1913.

Dorsey, Florence L. *Master of the Mississippi: Henry Shreve and the Conquest of the Mississippi.* Boston: Houghton Mifflin, 1941.

Duer, William. *New York As It Was.* New York: Stanford & Swords, 1849.

Flexner, James T. *Steamboats Come True.* New York: The Viking Press, 1944.

Gould, Emerson W. *Fifty Years on the Mississippi.* St. Louis: Nixon-Jones Printing Co., 1889.

Hamlin, Talbot. *Benjamin Henry Latrobe.* New York: Oxford University Press, 1955.

Hamm, Margherita. *Famous Families of New York.* New York: G.P. Putnam's Sons, 1902.

Herrick, Francis Hobart. *Audubon the Naturalist,* 2 vols., New York and London: D. Appleton & Co., 1917.

Howe, Henry. *Historical Collections of the Great West.* Cincinnati: G.F. Tuttle, 1857.

Hulbert, Archer B. *The Ohio River.* New York: G.P. Putnam's Sons, 1906.

Hunter, Louis C. *Steamboats on the Western Rivers.* Cambridge: Harvard University Press, 1949.

Leahy, Ethel C. *Who's Who on the Ohio River.* Cincinnati: E.C. Leahy Publishing Co., 1931.

Lloyd, James T. *Lloyd's Steamboat Directory and Disasters on the Western Waters.* Cincinnati: J.T. Lloyd and Co., 1856.

Lorant, Stefan. *Pittsburgh: The Story of an American City.* Garden City, N.Y.: Doubleday, 1964.

Morrison, John. *History of American Steam Navigation.* New York: Stephen Daye Press, 1958.

North, Stirling. *The First Steamboat Voyage on the Mississippi.* Boston: Houghton Mifflin, 1962.

Pen Pictures of Early Western Pennsylvania, ed. John Harpster. University of Pittsburgh Press, 1938.

Quest for America, 1810–1824, ed. Charles L. Sanford, in *Documents in American Civilization* series. New York: New York University Press, 1964.

Semmes, John E. *John H.B. Latrobe and His Times.* Baltimore: The Norman Remington Co., 1917.

Tocqueville, Alexis de. *Journey to America,* tr. George Lawrence; ed. J.P. Mayer, New Haven, 1960.

Trollope, Frances (Mrs. T.A.). *Domestic Manners of the Americans*. London: Whittaker, Treacher & Co.; New York: reprinted 1832.

Roosevelt, Nicholas. *A Front Row Seat*. Norman: University of Oklahoma Press, 1953.

Twain, Mark (Samuel Clemens). *Life on the Mississippi*. New York: Harper & Bros., 1903.

Vitz, Carl. *The Steamboat Comes to the Ohio. Bulletin of the Historical and Philosophical Society of Ohio,* vol. 10, no. 3, Cincinnati, July, 1952.

Whittelsey, Charles B. *The Roosevelt Genealogy*. Hartford, 1902.

INDEX

CHRISTIAN HERALD ASSOCIATION AND ITS MINISTRIES

CHRISTIAN HERALD ASSOCIATION, founded in 1878, publishes The Christian Herald Magazine, one of the leading interdenominational religious monthlies in America. Through its wide circulation, it brings inspiring articles and the latest news of religious developments to many families. From the magazine's pages came the initiative for CHRISTIAN HERALD CHILDREN'S HOME and THE BOWERY MISSION, two individually supported not-for-profit corporations.

CHRISTIAN HERALD CHILDREN'S HOME, established in 1894, is the name for a unique and dynamic ministry to disadvantaged children, offering hope and opportunities which would not otherwise be available for reasons of poverty and neglect. The goal is to develop each child's potential and to demonstrate Christian compassion and understanding to children in need.

Mont Lawn is a permanent camp located in Bushkill, Pennsylvania. It is the focal point of a ministry which provides a healthful "vacation with a purpose" to children who without it would be confined to the streets of the city. Up to 1000 children between the ages of 7 and 11 come to Mont Lawn each year.

Christian Herald Children's Home maintains year-round contact with children by means of an *In-City Youth Ministry*. Central to its philosophy is the belief that only through sustained relationships and demonstrated concern can individual lives be truly enriched. Special emphasis is on individual guidance, spiritual and family counseling and tutoring. This follow-up ministry to inner-city children culminates for many in financial assistance toward higher education and career counseling.

THE BOWERY MISSION, located at 227 Bowery, New York City, has since 1879 been reaching out to the lost men on the Bowery, offering them what could be their last chance to rebuild their lives. Every man is fed, clothed and ministered to. Countless numbers have entered the 90-day residential rehabilitation program at the Bowery Mission. A concentrated ministry of counseling, medical care, nutrition therapy, Bible study and Gospel services awakens a man to spiritual renewal within himself.

These ministries are supported solely by the voluntary contributions of individuals and by legacies and bequests. Contributions are tax deductible. Checks should be made out either to CHRISTIAN HERALD CHILDREN'S HOME or to THE BOWERY MISSION.

Administrative Office: 40 Overlook Drive, Chappaqua, New York 10514
Telephone: (914) 769-9000